SALAD D...

Book and Lyrics by

DOROTHY REYNOLDS and JULIAN SLADE

Music by

JULIAN SLADE

SAMUEL   FRENCH

LONDON

NEW YORK TORONTO SYDNEY HOLLYWOOD

© 1961 BY DOROTHY REYNOLDS AND JULIAN SLADE
LYRICS COPYRIGHT 1954 BY FRANCIS, DAY AND HUNTER LTD

This play is fully protected under the copyright laws of the British Commonwealth of Nations, the United States of America, and all other countries of the Universal Copyright Convention.

All rights are strictly reserved.

It is an infringement of the copyright to give any public performance or reading of this play either in its entirety or in the form of excerpts without the prior consent of the copyright owners; or to copy any part of it by manuscript, typescript, photography, or any other means of reproduction.

SAMUEL FRENCH LTD, 52 Fitzroy Street, London W1P 6JR, or their authorized agents, issue licences to amateurs to give performances of this play on payment of a fee. **A quotation will be given on application to us, or to our authorized agents.**

Licences are issued subject to the understanding that it shall be made clear in all advertising matter that the audience will witness an amateur performance; and that the names of the authors of plays shall be included in all announcements and on all programmes.

The publication of this play must not be taken to imply that it is necessarily available for performance by amateurs or professionals, either in the British Isles or overseas. Amateurs intending production must, in their own interests, make application to Samuel French Ltd or their authorized agents for consent before starting rehearsals or booking a theatre or hall.

ISBN 0 573 08025 9

SALAD DAYS

Produced by Linnit and Dunfree Ltd and Jack Hylton, by arrangement with J. A. Gatti, the Bristol Old Vic production, at the Vaudeville Theatre, London, on the 5th August 1954, with the following cast of characters:

(in the order of their appearance)

THE TRAMP	*Newton Blick*
JANE	*Eleanor Drew*
TIMOTHY	*John Warner*
DONS	*Dorothy Reynolds*
	Yvonne Coulette
	Christine Finn
	Pat Heywood
	Michael Aldridge
	James Cairncross
	Michael Meacham
	Joe Greig
TIMOTHY'S MOTHER	*Dorothy Reynolds*
TIMOTHY'S FATHER	*Michael Aldridge*
AUNT PRUE	*Pat Heywood*
LADY RAEBURN	*Yvonne Coulette*
HELOISE	*Dorothy Reynolds*
ASSISTANT	*Christine Finn*
MANICURIST	*Pat Heywood*
P.C. BOOT	*Joe Greig*
ROWENA	*Pat Heywood*
THE BISHOP	*Newton Blick*
TROPPO	*Bob Harris*
A BUTTERFLY CATCHER	*Michael Aldridge*
AN ARTIST	*Yvonne Coulette*
A SUNBATHER	*Dorothy Reynolds*
A TENNIS PLAYER	*Christine Finn*
FOSDYKE	*Michael Meacham*
SIR CLAMSBY WILLIAMS	*James Cairncross*
INSPECTOR	*Michael Aldridge*
NIGEL	*Michael Meacham*
AMERICAN	*Newton Blick*
SHOPGIRL	*Christine Finn*
THEATREGOERS	*Yvonne Coulette*
	James Cairncross
LADY	*Dorothy Reynolds*
MANAGER	*James Cairncross*
PIANIST	*Angus Mackay*
FIONA	*Christine Finn*
TOM SMITH	*Newton Blick*
WAITRESS	*Pat Heywood*
SLAVE	*Bob Harris*
ARMS DANCERS	*Yvonne Coulette*
	John Warner

Augustine Williams	*Michael Aldridge*
Asphynxia	*Dorothy Reynolds*
Pressmen	*Newton Blick*
	James Cairncross
Ladies	*Dorothy Reynolds*
	Yvonne Coulette
	Pat Heywood
Ambrose	*Michael Aldridge*
Marguerite	*Yvonne Coulette*
Anthea	*Dorothy Reynolds*
Electrode	*Joe Greig*
Uncle Zed	*James Cairncross*

Directed by Denis Carey

Musical Numbers staged by Elizabeth West

Décor by Patrick Robertson

SYNOPSIS OF SCENES

ACT I

Scene 1   The University
Scene 2   The Breakfast-room
Scene 3   The Park
Scene 4   The Beauty Parlour

Scene 5   The Park
Scene 6   The Foreign Office
Scene 7   The Inspector's Office
Scene 8   The Park

ACT II

Scene 1   The Night Club
Scene 2   Night Frontcloth
Scene 3   The Park Café Terrace
Scene 4   Frontcloth
Scene 5   The Dress Shop
Scene 6   Frontcloth

Scene 7   The Park
Scene 8   Frontcloth
Scene 9   The Flying Saucer
Scene 10   Frontcloth
Scene 11   The Park

MUSIC

Overture

ACT I

No.	1	Opening Music		
No.	2	Opening Chorus	"The Things that are Done by a Don"	Jane, Timothy and Dons
No.	3	Duet	"We Said We Wouldn't Look Back"	Jane and Timothy
No.	4	Concerted	"Find Yourself Something to Do"	Father, Mother, Aunt Prue and Timothy
No.	5	Song	"I Sit in the Sun"	Jane
No.	6	Song and Dance	"Oh, Look at Me, I'm Dancing!"	Timothy and Jane
No.	6a	Reprise	"Oh, Look at Me, I'm Dancing!"	Jane
No.	7	Bishop's Dance		Bishop
No.	8	Reprise	"Oh, Look at Me, I'm Dancing!"	Ensemble
No.	9	Trio and Dance	"It's Hush-Hush"	Uncle Clam, Fosdyke and Timothy
No.	10	Dance, Song and Chorus	"Out of Breath"	Ensemble

ACT II

No.	11	Song	"Cleopatra"	Manager
No.	11a	Reprise		Fiona
No.	12	Song	"Sand in My Eyes"	Asphynxia
No.	13	Trio	"It's Easy to Sing"	Jane, Timothy and Nigel
No.	13a	Reprise	"It's Easy to Sing"	Jane, Fiona and Nigel
No.	14	Concerted	"We're Looking for a Piano"	Ensemble
No.	14a	Reprise	"We're Looking for a Piano"	
No.	14b	Reprise	"We're Looking for a Piano"	
No.	15	Song	"The Time of My Life"	Jane
No.	16	Trio	"The Saucer Song"	Jane, Timothy and Uncle Zed
No.	16a	Reprise	"The Saucer Song"	Jane, Timothy and Uncle Zed
No.	17	Duet	"We Don't Understand Our Children"	Timothy's Mother and Lady Raeburn
No.	18	Reprise	"Oh, Look at Me, I'm Dancing!"	Ensemble
No.	19	Reprise	"Oh, Look at Me, I'm Dancing!"	Ensemble
No.	20	Reprise	"We Said We Wouldn't Look Back"	Jane and Timothy

SALAD DAYS

ACT I

SCENE I

The University

The backcloth depicts the park-like grounds of the University with a view of the buildings in the distance. Immediately below the backcloth, a slightly raised path runs from R to L, fronted by a large, arched gateway. There are tree and stone column wings R and L.

OPENING MUSIC   No. 1

When the CURTAIN rises, the general lighting is dim, with a pool of light C, where the TRAMP is seated on a stool at his piano, playing, as if composing, "I Sit in the Sun". The piano, known as "Minnie", is a small, five octave, ornate, Victorian upright, mounted on four small wheels. It has two largish ornate oil lamps where there are usually candles, and there is a large lamp with red glass at one end. At the other end there are barrow-like handles. After a few moments, the TRAMP rises and props the stool on the shafts. The LIGHTS come up and the music swells.

LIGHTING CUE I

A MALE DON enters R. The TRAMP collects a coin from the DON who exits up R. A FEMALE DON enters L, dodges the Tramp and exits up L. The TRAMP pushes the piano off R, leaving the stage empty.

OPENING CHORUS   No. 2

"THE THINGS THAT ARE DONE BY A DON"

JANE, TIMOTHY *and* DONS

The music becomes dignified and processional.
Four MALE DONS enter up R and four FEMALE DONS enter up L. They are capped and gowned. They march ceremoniously on and group. The MEN are RC and the GIRLS are LC

TIMOTHY and JANE, wearing B.A. gowns are lead on up R and up L respectively by the last two DONS. They come down C and TIMOTHY stands R of Jane.

DONS.

Farwell! Farewell! Farewell!
Noble Bachelors of Art!
By dint of labour unabated
You have gradually graduated.
Farewell! Farewell! Farewell!
The time has come for us to part,
But ere you pass from our tuition
Hear one final word of admonition.

The following sequence is sung antiphonally, like a psalm. JANE and TIMOTHY are presented with their scrolls.

MUSIC

GIRLS.	When you go from this University into the world outside
MEN.	Remember to speak of us with loyalty and pride.
GIRLS.	If your abysmal lack of knowledge is exposed, do not attempt to shoot a
MEN.	Rude and ungrateful line about your tutor.
1ST MAN.	If somebody wishes to recall a speech from Shakespeare and asks you to quote it,
2ND MAN.	Quote it as I rewrote it.
GIRLS.	Above all you must correct and admonish
ALL.	Any slanderer who insists on affirming that dons are donnish.

TIMOTHY and JANE exchange sceptical glances. During the following verses the DONS execute lively movements and actions. JANE crosses and stands down R. TIMOTHY crosses and stands down L.

You clearly think there's nothing drearier
Than a poor old don.
Don't judge us by our grim exterior
That is all put on.
For if you should stray by chance one day
And come on a gaggle of dons at play
You then would say that an old M.A.
Is quite the gayest of the gay.

Refrain

Oh, the things that are done by a don!
We may look dry and dusty
But under the gown
You will find a clown
Who is game for anything lusty!
We play jokes that are academical,
Legal, classical, even chemical!
Oh, the things, the mad, mad things
That are done by a don, don, don.

MEN.	Dear old Potts! We all acknowledge He's the daredevil of the College. Look at the way he romps and roisters Swallowing oysters in the cloisters!

GIRLS.	The Principal, so people say, Had a whale of a time on Founder's Day, And, if we are to believe the rumour Nearly lost her sense of humour. Ha ha haha haha haha hah!

ALL.	Oh, the things that are done by a don Are things which a don didn't oughter. If you want to cram For a Latin exam Just visit our Latin Quarter.

| | | MUSIC |

MEN. **Turkish coffee—just for the smell of it.**
GIRLS. **Cocoa parties—just for the hell of it.**
ALL. **Oh, the things, the mad, mad things**
That are done by a don, don, don.

1ST MAN. **Didn't the porters think us odd,**
Doing a square dance in the Quad!
2ND MAN. **And all because you proved that Homer**
Wrote his books in a drunken coma.
A GIRL. **Wasn't it fun the day you found**
A Roman vase on the football ground.
A MAN. **And wasn't it one of my best caprices**
Kicking the grubby old thing to pieces.

ALL. **Ha-ha! Ha-ha! Ha-ha! Ha-ha! Ha-ha!**
Oh, the things that are done by a don!
1ST GIRL. **That night when I and the Warden**
Went out in a boat
In order to quote
The jolliest bits of Auden!
2ND GIRL. **Off to bed with Proust and Mallory!**
TWO GIRLS. **Holding hands in the minstrels' gallery!**
GIRLS. **Oh, the things, the mad, mad things,**
That are done by a don, don, don!

By this time they are all dancing with Bacchic abandon round TIMOTHY *and* JANE, *who are both amazed and amused by the whole proceeding.*

Oh, the things that are done by a don!
By Jiminy, what bravado!
Singing at dawn
On the croquet lawn
The madrigal from *The Mikado!*
All our pranks are quite unbeatable,
Many of them are unrepeatable!
Oh, the things, the mad, mad things
That are done by a don, don, don!
Oh, the things, the mad, mad things
That are done by a don, don, don.

The DONS *dance gleefully out up* R *and up* L, *leaving* TIMOTHY *and* JANE *standing on opposite sides of the stage. During the number they have been symbols of the departing graduate. Now they become individuals and notice each other properly for the first time.* JANE *moves to exit up* C.

TIMOTHY [*crossing to* L *of Jane up* C] **Jane!**
JANE [*stopping and turning*] **Hallo, Timothy.**

During the following speeches they move gradually down C.

TIMOTHY. **Hullo!**
JANE. **When are you leaving?**
TIMOTHY. **By the twelve forty-five.**
JANE. **Oh.** [*She pauses*] **I'm catching the one-twenty.**
TIMOTHY. **Oh. Good.**
JANE. **Why good?**
TIMOTHY. **I mean—it's a good train.**
JANE. **What are you going to do, Timothy?**
TIMOTHY. **Just go home, I suppose. My family has plans for me.**

MUSIC

JANE. **Bad luck. So has mine. Have you said all your good-byes?**

TIMOTHY. **Yes, I've seen everybody except you.**

JANE. **It's lucky we bumped into each other.**

TIMOTHY. **Yes.** [*With unexpected fatality*] **I don't suppose we shall ever bump into each other again.**

JANE [*laughing*] **Oh, Timothy, what nonsense! You know what London is. We shall be constantly bumping.**

TIMOTHY. **Even so—it always seems to be the way—once you've gone down.**

JANE. **Then we'll arrange to meet this minute. Would Wednesday of next week suit you?**

TIMOTHY [*slightly taken aback*] **Oh, well—I'm not sure. I . . .**

JANE. **Let's say eleven. Where? At your place?**

TIMOTHY [*recoiling*] **Oh, *no*! My mother would ask questions.**

JANE. **Do your people nag at you, too?**

TIMOTHY. **Yes. At breakfast.**

JANE. **Always at breakfast?**

TIMOTHY. **That's usually the time for concerted attacks.**

JANE. **I know.** [*She moves a step or two down* C]

TIMOTHY *follows Jane.*

Look, why don't we meet in the park? You know—the place where we once had a picnic.

TIMOTHY. **The day we cut the Shakespeare exam to go to the first night of** *Hamlet* **. . .**

JANE [*after a pause; with an air of discovery*] **Oh, Timothy, that seems** *years* **ago.**

TIMOTHY. **Yes. And you said Wednesday of next week, that seems years** *ahead*. **I hope I shall recognize you.**

JANE. **Do you realize, Tim, what we shall be leaving behind?**

TIMOTHY. **Shall we be** *able* **to leave it behind?**

DUET

No. 3

"WE SAID WE WOULDN'T LOOK BACK"

JANE *and* TIMOTHY

JANE.	**We'll never be able to break the spell,**
TIMOTHY.	**The magic will hold us still.**
JANE.	**Sometimes we may pretend to forget**
TIMOTHY.	**But of course we never will.**
	Three perfect years.
JANE.	**Perhaps there'll be more,**
	Life's only beginning, you know.
TIMOTHY.	**Oh, yes, it's not that I want to stay—**
	It's just that I don't want to go.
JANE.	**We mustn't look back,**
TIMOTHY.	**No, we mustn't look back.**
BOTH.	**Whatever our memories are**
	We mustn't say these were our happiest days,
	But our happiest days so far.
JANE.	**If I start looking behind me**
	And begin retracing my track,
	I'll remind you to remind me
	We said we wouldn't look back.

MUSIC

TIMOTHY.   **And if you should happen to find me**
With an outlook dreary and black,
I'll remind you to remind me
We said we wouldn't look back.

BOTH.   **It's hard to forget the plays, the dances,**
The walks by the river in Spring,
The dons we've placated,
The lectures we missed
But soon they won't mean a thing.
So if I let nostalgia blind me
And my resolution is slack,
I'll remind you to remind me
We said we wouldn't look back.

JANE [*spoken*] **The quad's going to look awfully bare after we've gone.**
TIMOTHY [*spoken*] **We shall visit it and think it looks much smaller.**
JANE. **Who do you suppose will give all the parties?**
TIMOTHY. **There won't** *be* **any parties.** [*He sings*]

            They're certain to miss us when we've gone,
They're not worth much if they don't.
JANE.   **And they'll beg us to visit them time after time.**
Oh, dear! Maybe they won't.

TIMOTHY.   **But if I once start looking behind me**
And begin retracing my track,
I'll remind you to remind me
BOTH.   **We said we wouldn't look back.**
We've broken the ties
We've said the good-byes,
There's no more for us to pack.
Don't turn round
We're outward bound
And we said we wouldn't look back.
We said we wouldn't look back.

> JANE *and* TIMOTHY *walk slowly up* C *and turn round for a last look as—*
> *the* LIGHTS *dim to* BLACK-OUT

LIGHTING CUE 2

SCENE 2

The Breakfast-room

The setting is a window flat down C, *backed by black drapes. In front of the window there is a round table set with breakfast.*

CONCERTED NUMBER   No. 4

"FIND YOURSELF SOMETHING TO DO"

FATHER, MOTHER, AUNT PRUE *and* TIMOTHY

LIGHTING CUE 3

When the LIGHTS *come up, Timothy's* FATHER, MOTHER *and* AUNT
PRUE *enter on the musical introduction, each carrying a chair. They set the
chairs at the table and sit on the last beat of the introduction.* MOTHER
sits C, *above the table,* FATHER *sits* R *of it and* AUNT PRUE *sits* L *of it.*

FATHER *and* MOTHER [*over the music*]
            Timothy's late. Timothy's late.

FATHER. It's well after nine.

AUNT. It's twenty to eight.

FATHER. Your watch is wrong, Aunt.

AUNT. It isn't wrong, yours is.

MOTHER. He's later each day, can you guess what the cause is?

FATHER. Timothy's lazy. Timothy's days
Are spent in reclining.

AUNT. It's only a phase.

MOTHER. Some marmalade, Aunt? Or will you have honey?

FATHER. It's certainly time he was earning some money.
[*He reads his newspaper*]

MOTHER. Well, speak to him, darling, no time like the present.

AUNT. No need to be pompous, just pointed and pleasant.

FATHER. You do it.

MOTHER. No, you.

FATHER. Well, it won't matter who.

MOTHER *and* FATHER [*singing*]
If we can succeed in suppressing Aunt Prue.

The music continues. AUNT PRUE *drinks her tea.*

FATHER [*speaking*] Here he is.

MOTHER [*speaking*] Now, then. [*She rises and stands behind her chair*]

TIMOTHY *enters* L *and sits above the table. The following are sung on
ascending notes of a sustained chord.*

MOTHER. **Timothy!**

AUNT. **Timmy!**

FATHER. **Tim!**

FATHER, MOTHER, AUNT PRUE [*singing*]
Find yourself something to do, dear,
Find yourself something to do.
Choose a niche, a niche in which
You can nestle and know that it's you.
You'll be illustrious if you're industrious
What we are saying is true,
So find yourself something to do, dear,
Find yourself something to do, do, do, do, do, do,
Find yourself something to do.

AUNT PRUE *reads a comic paper.* MOTHER *stands* R *of Timothy.*

FATHER [*over the music*] Your uncles will help you, there's no need to worry.

MOTHER. Some tea, darling? [*She pours milk*]

TIMOTHY. Thank you.

MOTHER. We think you should hurry.
You've four willing uncles who'll give you attention.
[*She pours tea for Timothy*]

AUNT [*lowering her comic*]
There's five of them.

MOTHER *and* FATHER [*firmly*] *Four!* And the one we don't mention.

TIMOTHY *helps himself to sugar.*

MOTHER. There's dear Uncle Clam in that nice diplomatic . . .

AUNT. He's mad as a . . .

MOTHER. No, just a little erratic.

AUNT. He's mad as a hatter.

MOTHER.　　　　　　　　　　　　Well, that doesn't matter,
　　　　　He's willing to help us.
　　　　　[She crosses above Timothy to L of him and hits Aunt Prue with her newspaper]
　　　　　　　　　　　Now, Auntie, don't natter.

TIMOTHY picks up his cup.

FATHER.　　　There is Uncle Augustine—in Parliament, Tim.
AUNT.　　　A sticky old humbug, don't go and see him.

TIMOTHY drinks his tea.

FATHER.　　　There's General Sir Hector, the pride of the Army.
　　　　　He's bold and he's brave.
AUNT.　　　　　　　　　　　He's bald and he's barmy.
MOTHER.　　　There's dear Uncle Zed.
AUNT.　　　　　　　　　　Oh, I thought he was dead.
MOTHER and FATHER.
　　　　　Whatever has put such a thing in your head?
MOTHER.　　　So four of them, darling, who'd give you attention.
AUNT.　　　No, five of them.
MOTHER and FATHER.　　　　　Four! And the one we don't mention.
MOTHER.　　　Once more.
FATHER.　　　　　　　Altogether, now. [He rises]

AUNT PRUE rises.

MOTHER [singing] Timothy!
AUNT [singing]　　　　　Timmy!
FATHER [singing]　　　　　　　Tim!
FATHER, MOTHER AUNT PRUE [singing]
　　　　　Go and see Uncle Clam.
　　　　　[Spoken] Jam?
　　　　　Find yourself something to do.
　　　　　Then see Uncle Zed.
　　　　　[Spoken] Some bread?
　　　　　He'd do anything, darling, for you.
　　　　　See Uncle Hector, there's no-one correcter,
　　　　　See Uncle Augustine, too.

TIMOTHY takes out cigarettes and matches.

So find yourself something to do, dear
Find yourself something to do.
Do, do, do, do, do, etc.

TIMOTHY tries to strike a match.

Find yourself something to do.

TIMOTHY, on the last beat, succeeds in striking the match. MOTHER blows
it out as—

the LIGHTS dim to BLACK-OUT　　　　　　LIGHTING CUE 4

SCENE 3

The Park

There are small fenced trees up RC, *up* C *and up* LC. *Two park chairs stand* LC.

SONG   No. 5

"I SIT IN THE SUN"

JANE

When the LIGHTS *come up,* JANE *wanders in up* R, *humming. She is wearing the lightest of summer dresses, in contrast to her more severe clothes in Scene 1. She looks around her for Timothy, glances at her watch, then sings.*

LIGHTING CUE 5

JANE.   Timothy's late! Timothy's late!
             Never mind! I'm happy to wait.
             I've nothing to do. On a fine Summer day
             It's easy to while the time away.
             [*She moves to the chairs* LC]
             I ought to do as my mother said,
             And think of the men I might have wed,
             But now I'm happy, now I'm free,
             And the Summer sun's enough for me.
             [*She sits on the upstage chair* LC]

             I sit in the sun
             And one by one
             I collect my thoughts and think them over.
             Say to myself
             Sit tight on the shelf
             As long as you feel that you're in clover.
             Why be in haste?
             You've nothing to waste
             The best things come without rhyme or reason.
             Sit in the sun
             The sun, the sun,
             And you might be in love by the end of the season.
             [*She rises*]
             There's Viscount A, and gay Lord B.
             And of course the Hon'rable Mister C.
             [*She crosses to* C]
             Whom have I missed from this glittering list?
             Surely there must be the one for me?
             [*She moves* LC]
             Why not do as the other girls do,
             And search for a man the Summer through?
             Call me a fool, but I'll follow the rule
             "Wait and your love will come to you."
             [*She sits on the upstage chair* LC]

MUSIC

I sit in the sun
And one by one
I forget the gentlemen I'm refusing.
One happy day
The Summer may
Provide an Adonis of my own choosing.
Maybe I'll wait
Till I'm too late
But I shall have waited for one good reason.
Here in the sun
The sun, the sun,
I might be in love by the end of the season.

JANE rises, looks about her, moves up LC, *sees Timothy off up* R, *waves and waves again.*

TIMOTHY wanders in up R, *engrossed in a book, and nearly bumps into the tree up* C.

TIMOTHY. **Sorry.** [*He turns and wanders down* C]

JANE moves and stands in Timothy's path. TIMOTHY *walks round her to* RC. JANE *follows him.*

JANE [*tapping Timothy on the shoulder*] **Excuse me.**
TIMOTHY [*moving* R] **That's quite all right.** [*He turns*] **Jane!**
JANE [*moving to* L *of him*] **I've been waiting for hours.**
TIMOTHY. **Oh, I'm sorry. I went to the wrong side of the park. The fact is, I was deep in this book.**
JANE [*nodding*] **You seemed to be.** [*She crosses and sits on the downstage chair* LC]
TIMOTHY [*following Jane*] **Yes. I've been thinking pretty deeply lately, Jane.** [*He puts the book on the upstage chair and sits on the ground beside Jane*]
JANE. **Really?** [*She is sympathetic, but amused and unhelpful*]
TIMOTHY. **It's about my future. Actually. All this sitting about in the park—it won't ...
Well, I feel—I feel I ought to—find myself something to do.**

JANE nods.

A sort—of *niche,* **where I can settle ...**
JANE. **Are your parents being troublesome?**
TIMOTHY [*surprised*] **Yes.**
JANE. **You had a bad breakfast?**
TIMOTHY. **How did you know?**
JANE. **I know the signs. They're on at** *me* **again, about getting married.**
TIMOTHY [*rising*] **It's ridiculous! You can't marry just anyone.**
JANE. **That's exactly what mother's afraid of. She's got a very exclusive list.**
TIMOTHY [*sitting on the upstage chair* LC; *gloomily*] *My* **mother's got a list of uncles.**
JANE. **Uncles?**
TIMOTHY. **Yes. She's arranging for me to see them. You see, I happen to have rather a lot of influential ones. I'm very fortunate.**
JANE. **Yes. I'm very fortunate, too. My mother's throwing a party for the eligibles—a sort of big dance affair.**
TIMOTHY. **And all the young men come? The ones who'd like to marry you?**
JANE. **The ones my mother would** *like* **to like to marry me.**
TIMOTHY. **I suppose they're all rich and handsome and clever.**
JANE. **Some of them are** *rich.*
TIMOTHY [*nodding*] **Yes.** [*He takes the book from under him*] **My uncles are rich, too.**
JANE. **Our situations are very much alike.**

TIMOTHY. **What can one do? One can't fight them.** [*He fingers the book*]

JANE. **No, but you can make them unnecessary.** [*She ponders*] **I take it you're not against work on principle?**

TIMOTHY. **Oh, no.** [*He puts the book on his knee*]

JANE. **What sort of job would you like, if you could choose?**

TIMOTHY [*reeling it off*] **Something adventurous, amusing, with a living wage, and** *temporary.* **Imagine being in the same job for life.**

JANE. **That's exactly how I feel about marriage. Except that I wouldn't mind it being permanent.**

TIMOTHY. **But someone you were in love with.**

JANE [*with studied casualness*] **Not necessarily.** [*She takes the book*] **I can imagine marrying some-one I was—fond of, and—used to; someone I'd known for—one—or two years, and who thought the same as I about things.**

TIMOTHY [*rising; violently*] **I say!**

JANE. **What?**

TIMOTHY [*crossing to* RC] **Oh, nothing.** [*He mops his brow*] **It seems to be getting hotter.**

JANE *rises and puts the book on her chair.*

JANE [*crossing to* L *of Timothy*] **I mean, if you're happy with someone** *without* **marriage, you might fall in love** *after.* **I've always thought that.**

TIMOTHY [*very deep in thought*] **Yes.**

JANE. **So you see,** *we* **want what** *they* **do, really.**

TIMOTHY. **They?**

JANE. **The parents. Only without all the** *fuss.* *You* **could just get a job, and** *I* **could just get married.**

TIMOTHY [*deep in thought*] **People do it every day.**

JANE. **Exactly. I could** *help* **you with the job, perhaps.**

TIMOTHY [*turning to her*] **And I could help you to . . .** [*He turns away*] **No, no, no. I had an idea just now. I . . .** [*He pulls himself together*] **If I just took the first job that came along, I'd be too** *busy* **to see the uncles.**

JANE. **Yes, Timothy! Yes!**

TIMOTHY. **I could tell the family afterwards, when I'd** *got* **the job.**

JANE [*with two steps towards him*] **Yes! Yes!**

TIMOTHY. **Gosh! Yes!**

JANE. **They'd forgive us. They're quite fond of us, really.**

TIMOTHY. **Yes. I say, Jane, would it help at all if you married** *me?*

JANE [*stepping back*] **Tim!**

TIMOTHY [*hurriedly*] **Only if it would help, Jane. Only if it would help.**

JANE [*embracing him*] **Darling . . .**

TIMOTHY. **I don't want to push myself on to you or anything, but it did occur to me just now . . .**

JANE [*stepping back*] **It's a lovely idea. And very clever of you.**

TIMOTHY. **Really?**

JANE [*with a step down stage*] **Yes, because it fulfils all the conditions; it's adventurous—and amusing . . .**

They laugh.

[*With a step up stage*] **And we might—you know, what I said—***after.*

TIMOTHY. **Fall in love.**

JANE. **Yes.**

TIMOTHY [*crossing to the chairs* LC; *a little breathlessly*] **Well, which shall we do first?**

JANE *follows Timothy.*

Get a job, or get married?

JANE. **Get married. It would be difficult asking for a day off so soon.**   MUSIC

TIMOTHY sits thoughtfully on the downstage chair LC.

Are you changing your mind?

The TRAMP *wheels the piano on* R *and stands it* C. *The piano has a cover over it.*

TIMOTHY. **No, I was thinking about the parents.**
JANE [*sitting on the upstage chair* LC] **Well, don't weaken. Remember, we tell them the very minute it's too late.**
TIMOTHY. **Phew! It *is* getting hotter.**

The TRAMP *goes down* R. JANE *and* TIMOTHY *peer at the piano.*

TRAMP. **Good morning.**
JANE. **Good morning. What is it?**
TIMOTHY. **A barrel-organ of some kind. How long does it take—getting married?** [*He takes out his glasses and polishes them*]

The TRAMP *sits on the permanent seat down* R, *pulls his hat over his eyes and seems to go to sleep.*

JANE [*rising and crossing to the piano*] **Special licence? I'll find out about that.** [*She looks at the piano*] **Seems the wrong sort of shape.**
TIMOTHY. **I suppose I could drive a taxi, just to start with.**
JANE. **You have to have qualifications.** [*She looks under the piano cover*]
TIMOTHY. **I've got a degree.**
JANE [*crossing and resuming her seat*] **It can't be a barrel-organ, it hasn't got a handle.**
TIMOTHY. **Perhaps it fits inside, like a gramophone.**
TRAMP [*without moving*] **It's a piano.**
JANE [*rising*] **I'm so sorry.**
TIMOTHY [*rising*] **I say! We *do* beg your pardon.**
TRAMP [*still without moving*] **Take the cover off.**
JANE. **What?**
TRAMP. **Take a look at it, if you like.**
JANE [*crossing to* R *of the piano*] **Thank you very much.**

TIMOTHY *crosses to* L *of the piano and assists* JANE *to remove the cover.*

TIMOTHY. **Oh, I say.**
JANE. **It's pretty.** [*She throws the cover off* R]
TRAMP. **Like it?**
JANE. **Very much.**

The TRAMP *takes out a packet of sandwiches and a bottle of beer from his pockets.*

TRAMP. **Want to look after it for a bit?** [*He eats*]
JANE. **Look after it?**
TRAMP. **For a month or so. You sounded as if you were looking for a job.**
JANE [*moving* RC] **A job! You mean you'd *pay* us to look after it?**
TIMOTHY [*moving* C *and admiring the piano*] **I'll take it on free of charge if it's going begging.**

JANE *moves to* R *of Timothy, nudges him then turns to the Tramp.*

JANE. **How much?**
TIMOTHY. **Jane! Don't be silly!**

TRAMP [*munching*] **Seven pounds a week.**

> TIMOTHY *and* JANE *look at each other. From now on they are tentative but very polite.*

JANE. **Wouldn't it be cheaper to leave it in the left luggage?**
TRAMP. **She's an open-air piano—she'd waste away in the left luggage.**

> TIMOTHY *and* JANE *look at each other.*

TIMOTHY. **Does she bring you in a good living?**
TRAMP. **So-so. Parks are usually profitable pitches. You'll find you add considerably to your seven pounds. No overheads, you see.**

> TIMOTHY *looks up absent-mindedly.*

TIMOTHY. **Oh, I see.**
TRAMP. **Sandwich?**
JANE [*crossing to* L *of the Tramp*] **Thank you.** [*She takes a sandwich*]

> TIMOTHY *moves to* R *of the piano.*

I expect you have to have a licence.
TRAMP [*interested*] **Expect you have. I've never discovered.**
TIMOTHY [*moving above the piano*] **Haven't you ever been run in?**

> JANE *moves* RC.

TRAMP. **Not so far. But mind they don't get** *you.*
TIMOTHY. **Me! But I haven't said I'll . . .**
JANE [*moving to* R *of Tim and nudging him*] **We'll talk about it later.** [*To the Tramp*] **Meanwhile, as you've got your piano here, would you give us the pleasure of hearing you play?**
TIMOTHY. **Oh, yes, please do.**
TRAMP [*rising*] **That's a fair request—you want to know the quality of the instrument.**
[*He crosses to* R *of the piano*]

> TIMOTHY *stands* L *of the piano.* JANE *crosses and stands down* L *of Timothy.*

I'll show you round. [*He opens the lid*] **Date of birth.**

TIMOTHY. **Oh, look, it's got an inscription.** [*He reads the inscription on the inside of the lid*] **"This piano was built by Daniel Miskin, Esquire, gentleman, for the Great Exhibition held in honour of Her Majesty in the year eighteen-fifty-one. On this occasion, Her Majesty was graciously pleased to praise the craftsmanship, and to remark in the hearing of many notable persons: 'You have made a piano, Mr Miskin.' Furthermore, with truly royal condescension, Her Majesty, before a large assembly of loyal subjects, danced a figure to the notes of this instrument, thus deepening the love of all her people." Oh, I say! Over a hundred years old!**
TRAMP. **Yes.** [*He puts his bottle in the piano, closes the lid, then goes to the stool, and moves it to* RC] **Stool.** [*He returns to the piano*] **Lamps for playing after dark; they simply eat oil. Can you trim a wick?**
JANE. **I think so.**

> TIMOTHY *touches the red lamp.*

TRAMP. **Rear light. Keyboard.** [*He opens the keyboard*] **Only five octaves, but I've usually found them sufficient.** [*He moves the piano to* RC] **Is there any special little thing you'd like me to play?**

> TIMOTHY *moves to the chairs* LC.

JANE [*crossing to* L] **No. We leave it to you.** [*She throws the remains of her sandwich off* L]

> TIMOTHY *sits on the upstage chair* LC *and puts his book and glasses on the ground beside the chair.* JANE *sits on the downstage chair. The* TRAMP *sits at the piano, flexes his fingers and plays.*

MUSIC
No. 6

SONG AND DANCE

"OH, LOOK AT ME, I'M DANCING"

JANE *and* TIMOTHY

When the music begins, JANE'S and TIMOTHY'S feet begin to move. They rise, dance and react according to the lyric.

JANE [*singing*]   What's happening? I can't sit still,
                  I stand, I walk, against my will.

TIMOTHY.   What's happening? What can this be?
                  My feet have got control of me.

JANE.   I can't control my legs and feet,
                  They misbehave on every beat,
                  I'm not so sure that I approve.
                  Is this a seemly way to move?

BOTH.   I've lost command, I'm swept away,
                  The feeling's odd but rather gay;
                  The music took me by surprise
                  I hadn't time to realize.
                  What's happening? What's happening?
                  What's happening to me?

JANE.   Oh, look at me! Oh, look at me! Oh, look at me!
                  I'm dancing!
                  I'm going on one foot instead of on two,
                  It isn't a thing I'm accustomed to do.

TIMOTHY.   Oh, look at me! Oh, look at me! Oh, look at me!
                  I'm dancing!
                  Now who would have thought I'd behave in this way?
                  It isn't a thing that I do every day.
                  It's nice for a change and I'm happy to say

BOTH.   I'm dancing, dancing, dancing!

TIMOTHY.   I'm going backwards instead of forwards
                  I'm spinning like a top.

JANE.   I'm going sideways, I'm going upwards
                  I doubt if I can stop.

TIMOTHY [*spoken*]   **Stop!**

BOTH.   Look at me! Oh, look at me! Oh, look at me!
                  I'm dancing!
                  My feet are so wayward they've got out of hand.
                  I leap in the air never hoping to land,
                  I'm gay and I'm breathless and jubilant and
                  I'm dancing, dancing, dancing.

The music continues for the dance.

JANE [*singing as she dances*]
                  Look at me! Oh, look at me! Oh, look at me!
                  I'm dancing.

BOTH.   I'm dancing, dancing, dancing.

They both fall to the ground C, breathless and laughing. JANE is RC. TIMOTHY is LC.

The TRAMP rises, turns, bows and exits R. TIMOTHY and JANE do not notice him go.

TIMOTHY. **Oh, my goodness!** [*He rolls over to* C]
JANE. **That was wonderful!** [*She rolls over to* R *of Timothy*]
TIMOTHY. **Well, if that's dancing, I've never danced before.**
JANE. **I didn't know you had it in you.**
TIMOTHY. **Nor I.**

> *They come close together and almost kiss, then break away, embarrassed, and rise.* TIMOTHY *moves* LC *and picks up his book and glasses.*

JANE [*looking* R] **Oh! Oh! Where is he?**
TIMOTHY. **What?**
JANE [*moving* RC] **He's gone.**
TIMOTHY [*putting the book and glasses on the upstage chair* LC] **Good Lord! Did you see him go?**
JANE. **No. How strange.**
TIMOTHY [*looking off* R] **He's nowhere in sight.**
JANE. **Do you think he's coming back?** [*She opens the lid of the piano and looks inside*]
TIMOTHY. **No—somehow. The piano's got that sort—of abandoned look.**

> JANE *takes a bundle of notes and a slip of paper out of the piano.*

JANE [*rushing to Timothy*] **Tim, look! Money!**

> TIMOTHY *takes the money and counts it.*

TIMOTHY. **Twenty-eight pounds.** [*He returns the notes to Jane*]
JANE. **Seven pounds a week for four weeks.**

> *They stare at each other.*

TIMOTHY. **What's that? A note or something?**
JANE [*reading the slip of paper*] **"You take over as from the first of the month. This is to prove that you are in lawful possession of my piano."**
TIMOTHY. **It can't prove it—it isn't signed.**

> JANE *moves* C.

Jane! [*He moves to her*] **Had you any idea he was serious?**
JANE [*moving up* L *of the piano*] **I wasn't sure.** [*She puts the note in the piano*]
TIMOTHY. **I think I was just humouring him. Well, we shall have to take it on now.**
JANE. **There's no doubt about our taking it on, is there?**
TIMOTHY. **None in the world.**
JANE [*rushing excitedly to Timothy*] **Oh, Timothy!** [*She hands the notes to Timothy*] **Put these in a safe place.**

> TIMOTHY *pockets the notes.*

The first of the month—we've just got time to get married first. [*Busily*] **Where shall we keep it?**
TIMOTHY. **We'll have to hide it.**
JANE. **Somewhere safe. I shall never sleep a wink.**
TIMOTHY. **We'll have to hire a garage.**
JANE [*with precision*] **A small, lock-up garage.**
TIMOTHY. **Jane, supposing we run into your mother?**
JANE [*moving up* L *of the piano*] **With the piano? We won't. She's under the dryer.**
TIMOTHY. **The dryer?**
JANE. **She's gone to the hairdressers. She'll be safe for hours.**
TIMOTHY [*moving down* C] **Oh, good! I say, Jane—do you think the piano will make** *everyone* **dance?**
JANE. **The way it made us?**
TIMOTHY. **Oh, my goodness! I can't wait to find out.**
JANE [*moving* C] **Try it on me again.**
TIMOTHY. **Now?**

JANE. **Quick! There's no-one about.**
TIMOTHY. **I expect it was him, not the piano.**
JANE [*pulling Timothy to the piano*] **Try!**
TIMOTHY. **I don't think I'm as good at it as he is.**
JANE. **Try, darling, try.**
TIMOTHY [*sitting at the piano*] **All right. What?**
JANE. **The thing** he **played.**
TIMOTHY. **By ear?** [*Trying*] **I don't think I—can—no, I can't.** [*He tries again*]

REPRISE   **No. 6a**

"OH, LOOK AT ME, I'M DANCING"

JANE

[*Over the music*] **Yes, I can. Yes, I can.**
JANE [*exclaiming as she dances*] **Oh, look at me! Oh, look at me! Oh, look at me! It's working!**
TIMOTHY [*shouting as he plays*] **I say, Jane, do you think it's only us?**
JANE [*spoken*] **No. It's the piano. Tim, look! I'm dancing, dancing, dancing!**

JANE *whirls round and round as—*

the LIGHTS *dim to* BLACK-OUT

LIGHTING CUE 6

SCENE 4

The Beauty Parlour

The scene is played downstage in front of black drapes or running tabs. A hairdresser's swivel chair is set C, *with a hair-dryer on a portable stand behind it. A trolley is up* L *of the chair, with a supply of hairdresser's and beautician's equipment, cosmetics, tissues, etc.*

LIGHTING CUE 7

When the LIGHTS *come up,* LADY RAEBURN *is sitting under the dryer, reading a copy of "The Tatler". She faces the audience, which is, as it were, a huge mirror in which she studies her appearance at intervals during the scene. After a moment, she lowers the paper, takes her head out of the dryer, makes faces at the "mirror", then, with a sigh, puts her head back in the dryer and looks at the paper. After a few moments, she lowers the paper.*

LADY RAEBURN [*calling*] **Heloise!** [*She pauses. With an aristocratic shriek*] **Heloise!**

HELOISE *enters* L, *carrying a telephone with the receiver off. It has a seemingly endless flex.* HELOISE *is the head of the Beauty Salon and has the wise, sad smile of someone who knows it all.*

Heloise, haven't you any other *Tatler* **but this? I've already been handed it by my dentist and my dressmaker. I'm sick of it. It's full of that Plunkett girl.** [*She looks at the telephone*] **Is it for me? Thank you.** [*She takes the receiver in her left hand*]

HELOISE *takes the paper from Lady Raeburn and puts the telephone on her lap.*

[*She tries to put the receiver to her ear and clonks it loudly on the dryer*] **Heloise, do take this thing off! I'm toasted, anyway.**

HELOISE *removes the dryer and exits with it* R.

That's better. [*Into the telephone*] **Hullo? . . . Margo, my dear, it's you. How lovely! However**

MUSIC

did you guess I was here? . . . Oh, *no*, my dear. I'm not made of money. I only come twice a week . . .   MUSIC

> HELOISE *enters* R, *crosses to Lady Raeburn and removes the hair net and cotton wool.*

How are you? . . . Oh, I'm *desperate*, dear, but desperate. I'm simply middle-aged with worry . . . [*To Heloise*] I think bring the hair a little further over the forehead today, Heloise. [*Into the telephone*] Seriously, dear, I am . . . It's about Jane . . . Oh, you know *Jane*. My little gairl . . . Yes—Dick's child . . . [*To Heloise*] I think I'd better have *everything* today, Heloise. I've got a very important luncheon.

> HELOISE *ties a towel, turban fashion around Lady Raeburn's hair.*

[*Into the telephone*] Well, you know I'm giving this ball for Jane, to launch her properly . . . Oh, Margo, I *did* tell you . . . Of *course* I want you to come . . . Oh, now, Margo, don't be silly. There will be several people there who are really quite a lot older than you. My mother, for instance . . . [*To Heloise*] Carry on with my face. I can talk at the same time.

> HELOISE *beckons off* L.
>
> The ASSISTANT *enters* L. *Together, they smother Lady Raeburn's face with cold cream.*

[*She talks blandly on, but occasionally gets a mouthful or eyeful of the cream. Into the telephone*] No, it's all right, dear, they're just going to do my face . . . [*She laughs girlishly*] Oh, Margo, no! It's you who never get any older. I'm sagging all over the place these days . . . [*To Heloise*] Aren't I, Heloise?

> HELOISE *smiles her sad smile. She and the* ASSISTANT *wipe off the cream.*

[*Into the telephone*] About Jane . . . Well, my dear, for a start she seems to have lost all interest in clothes. As you know, we go to Gusset Creations, and Ambrose says she hasn't been there for weeks . . . Well, it's too disheartening after all I've *done* for her. And she never gets her hair done . . . [*To Heloise*] Does she, Heloise? [*Into the telephone*] Well, of course, the girl simply looks a wreck . . . [*She leans forward to look at herself in the mirror*] I do think one owes it to oneself to make the very most of one's natural gifts . . .

> HELOISE *pulls Lady Raeburn back and massages her face, pulling and pushing it like pastry and slapping her cheeks. The* ASSISTANT *gazes wearily into mirror.*

Sometimes I wonder if I was *wise* to send her to the University. She dashes off at all hours of the day and never tells me where she's going . . .

> HELOISE *slaps Lady Raeburn's throat.*

Heaven knows what she *does*. I mean, what does a gairl *do* these days . . . [*To Heloise*] Heloise, I want my nails doing. They are simply disgusting—they're like a parlourmaid's.

> HELOISE *beckons off* L, *then massages Lady Raeburn's neck, sweeping her hands up her jaw.*

[*Into the telephone*] I—simply—don't know—*what's* come over her . . .

> HELOISE *slowly sweeps her hands down Lady Raeburn's jaw.*

Oh, *no!* Not *love!* Oh—I should—*know* . . .

> HELOISE *turns Lady Raeburn's head to* R *and* L. *The first time, the words miss the telephone.*

A mother always knows . . . I said—a mother—always knows . . .

> HELOISE *massages her shoulders.*

No, dear, I'm being massaged . . . Oh, you should try it. It's the most restful thing in the world . . .

> *The* ASSISTANT *thrusts Lady Raeburn forward in the chair and* HELOISE *pummels her back.*   MUSIC

> *The* MANICURIST *enters* L, *and crosses to* R *of Lady Raeburn. She carries a tray with manicure materials.*

[*To the Manicurist*] **What's that you're going to put on my nails today, child?**

> *The* MANICURIST *shows her a bottle.*

Ah! "Blood on the Moon."

> *The* MANICURIST *kneels down* R *of Lady Raeburn and sets to work on her right hand.*

[*Into the telephone*] **Do you know "Blood on the Moon", Margo? . . . Such a comforting little colour . . .**

> HELOISE *places a face pack mask on Lady Raeburn's face, lifting it every now and then but shaking her head sadly as she sees the result.*

As I was saying, I've got plans for Jane. Now, do you know Nigel Danvers? . . . Yes, that's right . . .

> HELOISE *removes the mask and wipes her fingers on it.*

The Earl was quite an intimate friend of mine. Well, Nigel's one of my *plans* **. . .**

> HELOISE *puts the mask on the trolley.*

[*She glances* R. *To Heloise*] **Gracious, look at the time. Do hurry, Heloise! You haven't started yet.**

> *The three specialists now set to work at double speed. The* ASSISTANT *takes rouge and a puff from the trolley, crosses to* R *of Lady Raeburn and taps the Manicurist on the shoulder. The* MANICURIST *rises and crosses to* L *of Lady Raeburn.* HELOISE *collects the mascara and brush from the trolley.*

[*Into the telephone*] **My dear, I must tell you—I'm lunching with Jack . . .**

> *The* MANICURIST *tries to secure Lady Raeburn's left hand.*

[*To the Manicurist*] **Ah! What are you doing? Silly girl!** [*She transfers the receiver to her right hand*]

> *The* MANICURIST *kneels* L *of Lady Raeburn and works on her left hand. The* ASSISTANT *rouges her.*

[*Into the telephone*] **No, not** *that* **Jack. The one I met at Angela's the other day . . . Oh, it's quite all right. I can talk quite freely, there's nobody here . . .**

> HELOISE, *the* ASSISTANT *and the* MANICURIST *stare for a moment into the mirror. The treatment is now drawing to a close.*

Oh, yes, he's very special . . .

> HELOISE *spits on to the mascara, applies it to Lady Raeburn's eyelashes, and then to her own. The* ASSISTANT *puts the rouge on the trolley and prepares a powder puff.*

Well, you know how I dread Angela's parties. I nearly wasn't going. But as soon as I entered the room, something just hit me—

> *The* ASSISTANT *dashes a huge puff full of powder full in Lady Raeburn's face. The telephone rings off* L.

> *The* MANICURIST *rises, picks up her tray and exits* L. *The* ASSISTANT *takes the receiver from Lady Raeburn, but holds it near her mouth.* HELOISE *puts the mascara on the trolley, seizes Lady Raeburn's hands and pulls them right above her head to massage them.*

—and after one or two drinks, I felt so *tense*—**my dear, I might have been on the rack. I felt taut as a ramrod the whole of the next day until I got to Heloise. She's a marvel. She can relax you better than anyone else I know . . .**

> *The* MANICURIST *enters* L *with a second telephone and holds it out to Lady Raeburn.*

[*To the Manicurist*] **Oh, for me?** [*She takes the receiver from the Assistant. Into the first telephone*] **Excuse** <u>MUSIC</u>
me, Margo, I'm wanted on the phone. Don't ring off, I shall be back. [*She takes the receiver
from the Manicurist*]

> The MANICURIST *exits* L. HELOISE *is powdering her face.*

[*Into the second telephone*] **Hullo? . . . Jack darling, I was just going to ring you . . . No, of course
I haven't forgotten . . . Oh, darling, yes, roses would be lovely,** [HELOISE *pinches her nose so that
her voice quacks*] **roses are always lovely. Just a minute, let me see how I look . . .**

> They all look into the mirror.

[*To Heloise*] **Oh, Heloise, what have you done to me? I look at least thirty. I shall have to
have the whole treatment all over again.**

> HELOISE *collects the cream from the trolley.* The ASSISTANT *rolls up her
> sleeves in preparation for the attack.*

[*Into the second telephone*] **Darling, I'm afraid I shall be the teeniest, weeniest bit late . . . No,
no, I've only got to slip on a hat and I'm ready . . .** [*Into the first telephone*] **Margo, are you still
there? . . .**

> HELOISE *applies a liberal dob of cream on Lady Raeburn's nose as—*

> *the* LIGHTS *dim to* BLACK-OUT

> > > LIGHTING CUE **8**

SCENE 5

The Park

The setting is as SCENE 3, *but there is only one park chair which is* RC.

> > > LIGHTING CUE 9

> When the LIGHTS *come up, it is bright sunshine and the birds are singing.*
> P.C. BOOT *enters up* L. *He is high-spirited and jaunty. He regards a tree
> and blows his police whistle. The bird replies accordingly.* BOOT *crosses
> slowly to* L *of the chair* RC, *looks off* R, *crosses to* L, *faces front and polishes
> a button.* ROWENA *enters up* L *and crosses to* RC. *She carries a dress box
> marked "Gusset Creations". As she crosses,* BOOT *turns and whistles to*
> ROWENA *who stops and turns to him.*

BOOT. **Lovely morning, Miss Rowena.**
ROWENA. **It's you, Constable Boot. I didn't realize. All you chaps look the same from
behind.**
BOOT. **But not from the front, I hope.**
ROWENA. **Oh, no, I'd know you anywhere—by your face. How are you?**
BOOT [*crossing to* L *of Rowena*] **Just in the mood for a nice arrest.**
ROWENA [*crossing to* LC] **Ooh! I don't think you're nice to know, having truck with criminals.**
BOOT [*crossing to* R *of Rowena*] **There's nothing to it, really. A man's life.**
ROWENA. **I wouldn't think it too familiar if you called me "Rowena".**
BOOT. **"Lancelot" 's my name.**
ROWENA [*impressed*] **Lancelot! Who'd have thought you had it in you?**
BOOT [*moving* C] **How's Gusset Creations? Still creating?**
ROWENA [*moving to* L *of Boot*] **Nicely, thanks. I'm out on a personal deliverance.**
BOOT. **You don't say! What is it?**
ROWENA. **It's a Gusset Creation in the latest shade of triple cinnamon and custard. It's
got a split lamé drape and—**[*with a gesture*] **buttons all the way up the back.**
BOOT. **Is it chic?**
ROWENA. **No. I think it's a bit common. It looked lovely in the window—but horrible on.**

BOOT. **Where's it for?**

ROWENA. **Curzon Street.**

BOOT. **You've come a long way round for your short cut.**

ROWENA [*crossing down* R; *swinging her box*] **I think I'm entitled to a bit of a stroll.**

BOOT [*moving to* L *of Rowena*] **Sure it wasn't so's you'd bump into me?**

ROWENA. **You think too much of yourself, Lancelot Boot.**

BOOT [*confident*] **Oh, come on.**

ROWENA [*crossing to* LC] **I'll take great care I don't bump into you again.**

BOOT [*moving to* R *of Rowena*] **Tuesday's my evening off.**

ROWENA. **There's plenty more policemen where you come from.**

BOOT. **Meet you at six pip emma.**

ROWENA. **You can whistle for me.**

BOOT. **Outside the** *Plaza.*

ROWENA. **Who's on?**

BOOT. **Gina Lollobridgewater.**

There is a pause. ROWENA *wavers and crosses down* R.

ROWENA [*finally*] **That'll be as may be, Lancelot.**

ROWENA *exits with a little kick down* R.

BOOT. **Lancelot.** [*He twirls*]

JANE *enters* R.

BOOT *twirls into Jane's arms, and embarrassed, hurriedly exits* L.

JANE [*calling off* R] **Come on.**

TIMOTHY *pushes the piano on* R.

TIMOTHY. **Here?**

JANE. **Yes.**

TIMOTHY [*pushing the piano to* LC] **Not too near the road and not too secluded.** [*He sets the stool in front of the piano*] **What's the time?**

JANE. **A quarter to ten. There aren't many people about yet.**

TIMOTHY. **Let's wait till there are a** *lot.*

JANE [*moving* C] **Or one or two choice ones.**

TIMOTHY [*excitedly*] **Oh, come on, choice ones.** [*He opens the piano lid*]

JANE [*moving above the piano*] **Do you think she's all right?**

TIMOTHY. **Minnie?**

JANE. **It isn't damp in that garage?**

TIMOTHY. **No. But if the weather breaks . . .**

JANE. **It won't.** [*She glances up* L] **Oh, quick, there's someone coming.**

TIMOTHY *sits at the piano and fingers the keys.*

No—[*she moves a little up* C] **they're taking the other path—I think.** [*She moves down* R *of the piano*] **Yes.**

They relax. TIMOTHY *spins on the stool and faces front.*

TIMOTHY. **Jane.**

JANE [*moving down* R *of Timothy*] **Yes?**

TIMOTHY. **It's no good, I shan't enjoy today unless I tell you. I've got an awful confession.**

JANE. **What is it?**

TIMOTHY. **I didn't break it to the family.**

JANE. **Tim!**

TIMOTHY. **Not about us, nor about Minnie. Mother forestalled me. She's made dates for me with two of the uncles—I shall have to go and see them.**

JANE. **I see.**

TIMOTHY. **It's weak of me, isn't it?**

JANE. **Yes.** [*She moves* C] **But I'm very relieved you're weak, because you see, I didn't tell my mother, either.**

TIMOTHY. **Jane!**

JANE [*kneeling* R *of Timothy*] **She's been so busy sending out invitations.**

TIMOTHY [*embracing her*] **How wonderful! You're as weak as I am. How wonderful!**

JANE. **It isn't wonderful. It'll get worse every day.**

TIMOTHY [*rising exultantly*] **I don't care.** [*He moves a little up* C]

JANE [*rising*] **And I shall have to go to the Eligibles' party.** [*She sits on the stool*]

TIMOTHY. **Never mind, you won't enjoy it.** [*He moves down* C] **I mean, they're all pretty awful, aren't they?**

JANE [*swinging round on the stool*] **No, one of them isn't awful. He's quite nice.**

TIMOTHY. **Who's quite nice?**

JANE. **Oh—just a young man. Nigel Danvers, his name is.**

TIMOTHY [*moving to* R *of Jane*] **You mean** *Lord* **Danvers?**

JANE. **Yes.**

TIMOTHY. **You don't like him** *very* **much, do you?**

JANE. **Would you mind?**

TIMOTHY. **I don't know. Since we got married I seem to have noticed you more.**

JANE. **Yes, it has rather thrown us together.**

TIMOTHY [*moving close to her*] **In fact, I think I could get quite serious about you, Jane.**

JANE [*half rising*] **Could you?** [*She resumes her seat, turns away, then turns back again to Tim*] **Who are the uncles?**

TIMOTHY [*squatting on the ground* R *of Jane*] **Uncle Clam, diplomatic—and Uncle Zed. He's the end.**

JANE [*rising excitedly*] **Look!**

> *The* BISHOP *enters up* R, *and comes down* C. *He is engrossed in a book.*
>
> JANE *and* TIMOTHY *watch, fascinated.*

[*She moves above the piano*] **Perfect!**

TIMOTHY [*sitting on the stool*] **It's like bird-watching!**

> *The* BISHOP *sits on the chair* RC.

JANE. **Sh!**

TIMOTHY [*whispering*] **Now?** [*He faces the keyboard*]

JANE. **Yes, now.**

> TIMOTHY *plays.*

BISHOP'S DANCE   No. 7

> *As* TIMOTHY *plays, the* BISHOP, *seated, begins to tap and kick his legs. Then he rises and dances. At the end of the dance, he is again seated on the chair* RC, *reading.* TIMOTHY *rises and moves* C. JANE *stands down* L *of Timothy.*
>
> TROPPO *enters up* R *as the Bishop subsides. He looks at Timothy and Jane then goes smartly to the Bishop and holds out his hat. The* BISHOP *automatically drops in half a crown.* TROPPO *crosses and offers the coin to Jane.*

TIMOTHY. **Half a crown! I say! Well done! We completely forgot about a hat.**

JANE [*to Troppo*] **Thank you very much for reminding us. You have the half-crown.**

> TROPPO *shakes his head, offers the coin again then puts it on the piano.*

You want us to have it?

> TROPPO *points to the piano.*

The piano?

> TROPPO *nods.*

[*She moves up* R *of the piano*] **Do you like her? Let me introduce you. This is Minnie.**

> TROPPO *crosses to the piano, "asks" for permission and plays a note.* TIMOTHY, JANE *and the* BISHOP *kick once.*

Timothy. **What's your name!**

Troppo *shakes his head.*

[*To Jane*] **Can't he talk?**

Jane [*moving to* L *of Timothy*] **He seems to manage without.** [*To Troppo*] **Did the piano make you dance?**

Troppo *nods eagerly, skips a few steps then mimes that he will take round the hat.*

You'd collect for us?

Troppo *nods.*

Timothy. **Why not?**

Jane [*to Troppo*] **Would you like a job?**

Troppo *nods.*

Timothy. **Done!** [*To Jane*] **How much shall we pay him?**

Jane [*reckoning*] **Two pounds six and eightpence.**

Troppo *shakes his head violently.*

Timothy. **Not enough?**

Troppo *shakes his head.*

Jane [*inspired*] **Too much?**

Troppo *nods.*

Timothy. **I don't think he quite understands.** [*To Troppo*] **You really mean it's too much?**

Troppo *nods.*

Jane. **You'll be very useful—you can look after Minnie. She'll be safe with you.**

Troppo *makes a gesture as if guarding the piano with his life.*

Timothy. **Let's see how much we collect and then have a share out.**

Jane [*crossing to* R *of Troppo*] **Meanwhile, you look after the collection, will you?**

Troppo *nods.*

Where do you live?

Troppo *shakes his head.*

You don't live anywhere?

Troppo *shakes his head.*

[*To Timothy*] **The garage?**

Timothy. **Is that allowed?**

Jane. **Till they find out. I could bring some things.** [*To Troppo*] **Would you like to live with Minnie?**

Troppo *responds eagerly.*

Timothy. **Done!** [*He looks up* C] **Oh, look! Jane, people coming.**

Jane *and* Troppo *move* L. Timothy *sits at the piano and plays.*

REPRISE   No. 8

"OH LOOK AT ME, I'M DANCING"

Ensemble

Several Passers-by *enter, including* Rowena, *a* Butterfly Catcher, *an* Artist, *a* Sunbather, *a* Tennis Player *and* Fosdyke. *They severally or together dance in a variety of styles. The* Bishop *rises and joins in, along with* Jane *and* Troppo.

Boot *enters* R *and makes a brief attempt to create order, then joins the dancing in a prominent position.*

ALL [*shouting and singing*]　　　　　　　　　　　　　　　　

>Look at me! Look at me! Look at me!
>Look at me! Look at me! Look at me!
>Look at me! Look at me! Look at me!
>Look at me! Look at me! I'm dancing!
>Oh, look at me! Oh, look at me! Oh, look at me!
>I'm dancing!
>My feet are so wayward they've got out of hand
>I leap in the air, never hoping to land.
>I'm gay and I'm breathless and jubilant and
>I'm dancing, dancing.

>*The music continues as—*
>
>*the* RUNNING TABS *close*
>
>*The* CHORUS *dance on* R *in front of the* RUNNING TABS.

ALL [*singing*]

>Oh, look at me! Oh, look at me! Oh, look at me!
>I'm dancing!
>I'm going on one foot instead of on two,
>It isn't a thing I'm accustomed to do.
>Oh, look at me! Oh, look at me! Oh, look at me!
>I'm dancing!
>Now who would have thought I'd behave in this way?
>It isn't a thing I do every day.
>It's nice for a change and I'm happy to say,
>I'm dancing, dancing, dancing!
>
>I'm going backwards instead of forwards,
>I'm spinning like a top.
>I'm going sideways, I'm going upwards,
>I doubt if I can stop.
>Oh, look at me! Oh, look at me! Oh, look at me!
>I'm dancing!
>My feet are so wayward they've got out of hand,
>I leap in the air never hoping to land.
>I'm gay and I'm breathless and jubilant, and
>I'm dancing, dancing, dancing!

>*The* CHORUS *dance off* L *as—*
>
>*the* LIGHTS *dim to* BLACK-OUT

LIGHTING CUE 10

MUSIC

SCENE 6

The Foreign Office

There is a flat-topped desk R *with an office chair behind it and a large safe up* L, *with a combination lock.*

LIGHTING CUE 11

When the RUNNING TABS *open, the* LIGHTS *come up.* SIR CLAMSBY WILLIAMS *enters* L. *He tiptoes towards the audience, puts his finger to his lips, then moves* R *and hangs his hat and umbrella on a hat-stand which appears from the wings* R *and disappears again. He creeps to the safe and, after elaborate convolutions of the locks, opens it. He glances surreptitiously around then brings out a tea tray with teapot, cups, etc. He puts the tray on the desk and takes a flower from a vase on the desk, and speaks into it.*

UNCLE CLAM [*in a low voice*] **Fosdyke. Come in a moment, please.** [*He replaces the flower then pours tea*]

FOSDYKE, *a dignified attaché, enters* L, *very out of breath.*

FOSDYKE. **Yes, Sir Clamsby?**

UNCLE CLAM. **You're very puffed, Fosdyke. What have you been doing?**

FOSDYKE. **Sh!**

UNCLE CLAM. **Sh! It's all right, Fosdyke, you can tell me.** [*He crosses to* R *of Fosdyke*] **Go on. Please.** [*He puts his ear near Fosdyke*] **Oh, all right, then—whisper.**

FOSDYKE [*whispering*] **Dancing in the park.**

UNCLE CLAM [*loudly*] **Dancing in the park?** *Sh!*

FOSDYKE. **Sh!**

UNCLE CLAM. **Fosdyke, whatever can have caused you to commit such an indiscretion? What was it that made you dance?**

FOSDYKE [*scarcely audible*] **A piano.**

UNCLE CLAM [*loudly*] **A piano!**

FOSDYKE
UNCLE CLAM }[*together*] **Sh!**

UNCLE CLAM. **Ah, pianissimo! Fosdyke, you must not reveal one word of this to anyone. Understand?**

FOSDYKE *draws himself up, removes his hat and holds it over his heart.*

FOSDYKE. **The piano shall go with me to the grave.** [*He puts on his hat*]

UNCLE CLAM. **Will there be room?** [*He moves and sits above the desk*] **Listen, Fosdyke, we're expecting a visitor here this afternoon.**

FOSDYKE [*moving to* L *of the desk*] **May one ask whom?**

UNCLE CLAM. **Sh!**

FOSDYKE. **Sh!**

UNCLE CLAM [*with extreme caution*] **My nephew Timothy.**

FOSDYKE *nods eagerly.*

We must take the usual safety precautions, Fosdyke. Put the papers in the safe. [*He rises*]

FOSDYKE [*picking up some papers from the desk*] **Ah, yes. The safe.**

UNCLE CLAM *and* FOSDYKE *put the papers in the safe.* FOSDYKE *bangs the door on Uncle Clam's fingers.*

UNCLE CLAM [*yelling*] **Oh!**

FOSDYKE. **Sh!**

UNCLE CLAM. **Sh!** [*He sits at the desk in a diplomatic attitude*]

FOSDYKE *stands behind Uncle Clam. There is a knock off* L.

[*He calls*] **Come in.**

TIMOTHY *enters* L *and crosses to* C.

[*He rises and crosses to Timothy*] **Ah, my dear Timothy.**
TIMOTHY [*shaking hands with Uncle Clam*] **Hullo, Uncle Clam. How are you?**

UNCLE CLAM *and* FOSDYKE *exchange horrified glances.*

UNCLE CLAM. **Don't ask dangerous questions. You know my attaché—Fosdyke?**
TIMOTHY. **Your attaché?**
UNCLE CLAM. **Yes, he's quite a case.**
FOSDYKE. **How do you do?** [*He moves* R *and is handed a chair from the wings*]
TIMOTHY. **How do you do?**

FOSDYKE *crosses and sets the chair* LC.

No, I don't think we have met. Wait a minute. Your face does look vaguely familiar. [*He moves to* R *of Fosdyke*] **I know—haven't I seen you dancing . . . ?**

UNCLE CLAM *claps his hand over Timothy's mouth.*

FOSDYKE. **Sh!**
TIMOTHY. **I had no idea one had to be so cautious.**
UNCLE CLAM [*with a patronizing laugh*] **Cautious? You must learn to conceal** *everything*—**even the things you don't know.** [*He sits at the desk and pours a cup of tea for Timothy*]
TIMOTHY [*thinking this over*] **Oh.**
UNCLE CLAM. **Tea?**

FOSDYKE *crosses to* L *of Uncle Clam.*

TIMOTHY [*sitting on the chair* LC] **Please.**
UNCLE CLAM. **Sugar?**

FOSDYKE *and* UNCLE CLAM *look expectantly at* TIMOTHY, *who rises, goes to the safe, looks behind it, glances around to make sure he is not overheard, then resumes his seat.*

TIMOTHY [*in a whisper*] **Yes.**
UNCLE CLAM. **Excellent, Nephew. You will make a superb diplomat.**

FOSDYKE *takes the cup of tea to Timothy.*

TIMOTHY. **It must be very exciting to know everything and to reveal nothing.**

FOSDYKE *takes Timothy's hat and puts it on the safe.*

UNCLE CLAM. **Know everything?** [*He rises and stands* L *of the desk*] **My dear boy, whatever gives you that idea?**
TIMOTHY. **Surely you hold the secrets of all the nations?**

FOSDYKE *moves to* R *of the desk.*

UNCLE CLAM. **No, no! We only** *pretend* **to. That is what is meant by diplomacy.**

TIMOTHY'S *face falls.*

Oh, I can see you're disappointed.

The hat-stand appears R. FOSDYKE *takes Uncle Clam's hat and umbrella from it, hands them to Uncle Clam then goes down* R.

You had hoped you might become a swayer of destinies. [*He sighs*] **So did I, once upon a time.**

TRIO AND DANCE

"IT'S HUSH-HUSH"

UNCLE CLAM, FOSDYKE *and* TIMOTHY

No. 9

During the introduction, UNCLE CLAM *climbs on to the desk.* TIMOTHY *rises, crosses to* L *of the desk and puts down his cup.* FOSDYKE *stands* R *of the desk.*

MUSIC

UNCLE CLAM.	When I was given this high position I pictured myself, poor fool that I was, As a wise, all-powerful magician, A sort of political Wizard of Oz. "At last", I thought, "I'll know for certain What diplomacy really means, I'll soon ring up that Iron Curtain, I'll soon be seen behind the scenes." But all my jobs appeared to consist of, Much to my chagrin and dismay, Was a painfully comprehensive list of Things I must never do or say.
	Don't ever ask what job you're on It's Hush-Hush. Don't ever ask where the Empire's gone It's Hush-Hush. If you invent a code that's new Nobody must be able to Decipher the code—not even you. It's Hush-Hush.
UNCLE CLAM *and* FOSDYKE.	Your safes must be safe as rocks And baffle all investigations.
FOSDYKE.	Double-cross your double locks
UNCLE CLAM.	And keep on changing your combinations.
UNCLE CLAM *and* FOSDYKE.	Always travel in darkened specs, Use a cross to sign your cheques, And never reveal your age or sex,
ALL.	It's hush-hush, hush-hush, hush-hush, hush-hush, hush-hush, Hush-hush, hush-hush, hush-hush, hush-hush, hush-hush.

They dance and come down to the footlights. The RUNNING TABS *close behind them.*

UNCLE CLAM.	Don't ever ask who won the war
ALL.	It's Hush-Hush.
FOSDYKE.	Don't ever ask what the war was for
ALL.	It's Hush-Hush.
UNCLE CLAM *and* FOSDYKE.	If a foreigner comes to stay (Especially from the U.S.A.) Don't ever say "What a lovely day",
TIMOTHY.	It's Hush-Hush.
UNCLE CLAM *and* FOSDYKE.	When you go to a foreign shore Take, to give you a certain cachet,
FOSDYKE.	The briefest case you ever saw
UNCLE CLAM.	And also a semi-detached attaché.
TIMOTHY [*spoken*]	How do you do?
FOSDYKE [*spoken*]	Not at all.
ALL.	At Russian teas, lest you forget And make a remark you might regret Write on a Soviet serviette Necrasniette. Hush-Hush, hush-hush, hush-hush, hush-hush, Hush-hush, hush-hush, hush-hush, hush-hush, hush-hush.

They dance.

MUSIC

If you are knighted by and by,
Accept the honour, don't be shy,
But don't even try to find out why.
It's hush-hush, hush-hush, hush-hush, hush-hush,
Hush-hush, hush-hush, hush-hush, hush-hush, hush-hush.
Hush! Hush! Hush!

They exit L *as—*

LIGHTING CUE 12

the LIGHTS *dim to* BLACK-OUT

SCENE 7

The Inspector's Office

There is a high desk LC, *and a gramophone up* RC.

LIGHTING CUE 13

When the RUNNING TABS *open, the* LIGHTS *come up. The* INSPECTOR *is standing at the desk, making entries in a large book. There is a knock off* L.

INSPECTOR [*calling*] **Come in.**

BOOT *enters up* L *and crosses to* C. *He is very worried. As he crosses, he trips, falls on his face, rises, then salutes and hits himself in the eyes.*

Yes?

BOOT [*standing to attention*] **Constable Boot to make a report, sir.**
INSPECTOR [*absorbed in his writing*] **What do you wish to report, Boot?**
BOOT. **Offence in the park, sir.**
INSPECTOR. **What sort of a fence?** [*He makes notes*]
BOOT. **I'm here to investigate its nature, sir.**
INSPECTOR. **Was it a wooden fence?**
BOOT. **"Offence", sir, not a fence.**
INSPECTOR. **A fence, yes. Did you examine it?**
BOOT. **Not clearly, sir.**
INSPECTOR. **Fog?**
BOOT. **No, sir—mobile. Oh, it led me such a dance, sir.**
INSPECTOR. **The fence did?**
BOOT [*clearly*] **"Offence", sir.**
INSPECTOR. **I heard you. Where was it?**
BOOT. **Come and gone, sir.**
INSPECTOR. **Now, let's be accurate, Boot. Mobile, I think you said.**
BOOT. **No, sir. It was me that was mobile, sir.**
INSPECTOR. **Ah! You were attempting to locate the fence?**
BOOT [*loudly*] **"Offence", sir.**
INSPECTOR. **I'm not deaf. Did you locate the fence?**
BOOT. **I was in no position to, sir.**
INSPECTOR. **Why? What** *was* **your position?**
BOOT. **This, sir.** [*He takes up an attitude as for a Scottish jig*]
INSPECTOR. **Ah! You were** *climbing over* **the fence.**
BOOT [*moving to the desk*] **Do you mind if I write it down, sir?**
INSPECTOR [*interested*] **Indecent?**
BOOT [*shouting as he writes*] **No—"offence".**
INSPECTOR [*shouting*] **None taken.**

BOOT *flinches and points to the book.*

[*He looks at the book*] **Oh—"offence". I thought you said a "fence".** [*He laboriously crosses out his* *previous notes*]

BOOT *crosses to* C *and stands to attention.*

What sort of an offence was it?

BOOT. **I'm here to investigate its nature, sir.**

INSPECTOR. **"Mobile", I think you said.**

BOOT. **No, sir. That was me, sir.**

INSPECTOR. **You'd better relax, Boot.**

BOOT [*relaxing*] **Thank you, sir.** [*He removes his helmet and puts it on the desk*]

INSPECTOR. **Now then, from the beginning. Accuracy, Boot. "I was on my beat when . . ."?**

BOOT [*gratefully*] **Thank you very much, sir. I was on my beat when I heard music . . .**

INSPECTOR. **Ah! You were in the bandstand . . .**

BOOT. **No, sir. There was only one piano.**

INSPECTOR [*writing*] **Solo musical instrument.** *Grand* **piano.**

BOOT. **Mini, sir.**

INSPECTOR. **Who?**

BOOT. **Minipiano, sir.**

INSPECTOR. **What?**

BOOT. **On wheels, sir.**

INSPECTOR. **Ah, a vehicle. You said a musical instrument.**

BOOT. **No,** *you* **did, sir.**

INSPECTOR [*sharply*] **Attention, Boot.**

BOOT *jumps to attention.*

Now, from the beginning. Accuracy, Boot. Was it a musical vehicle, or a vehicular instrument?

BOOT. **Call it an instrument, sir.**

INSPECTOR [*writing*] **Unlawful musical vehicular instrument—you mean it wasn't licensed?**

BOOT. **I was in no position to enquire, sir.**

INSPECTOR. **Why? What position . . . ?**

BOOT *takes up an attitude like a Greek dancer.*

BOOT. **This, sir.**

INSPECTOR. **Did anyone notice you in that position?**

BOOT. **I don't think so, sir. The bystanders were all dancing.**

INSPECTOR [*elated*] **Dancing!** [*He moves to* L *of Boot*] **In the park! You didn't arrest them?**

BOOT. **No, sir. I also was a victim of the momentum.**

INSPECTOR. **Dancing! In the park! Now, don't hurry, Boot. Accuracy. Dancing's a bit of a hobby of mine.** [*Decisively*] **You were dancing. In what style?**

BOOT. **Sir?**

INSPECTOR. **What steps were you using?**

BOOT. **Miscellaneous, sir.**

INSPECTOR [*crossing to the gramophone*] **That won't do for the report.** [*He winds the gramophone and puts on a record*] **We'll have to take steps to find out. Know these records? I've got quite a collection. Attention, Boot.**

BOOT. **Sir.** [*He collects his helmet and puts it on*]

The INSPECTOR *starts the gramophone. The music, a tango, is played off* R.

INSPECTOR. **You be the lady—I'm taller.**

They dance an exaggerated tango.

[*He stops*] **Anything like that?**

BOOT. **No, sir.**

INSPECTOR [*moving to the gramophone*] **What a pity.** [*He changes the record*] **Well, let's have a bash** MUSIC **at this.** [*He starts the gramophone*] **I'll lead, you follow.**

They dance a quick-step.

[*During the dance*] **Lovely floor, isn't it? Do you come here often?** [*After an elaborate turn which lands them close together*] **Getting familiar?**

BOOT. **I think we're on the wrong track, sir.**

INSPECTOR [*stopping*] **Perhaps you were fox-trotting?** [*He stops the gramophone*]

BOOT. **Perhaps so, sir.**

INSPECTOR. **Well, show me. I can follow.**

BOOT. **But I wasn't being a lady, sir.**

INSPECTOR. **You were being a gentleman.**

BOOT. **I hope so, sir. I mean, I was dancing by myself.**

INSPECTOR [*crossing to the desk*] **Oh, well, why didn't you say so before?** [*He writes*] **"Officer on duty** *pas seul.*" *Quel* **period—what period?**

BOOT. **Sir?**

INSPECTOR. **Look, I'm an authority. Show me.**

BOOT. **Oh, I see what you mean, sir. Well, I think I jigged.**

INSPECTOR. **Irish jig. Well, go on.** [*He makes notes as Boot dances*]

BOOT *dances. For the rest of the scene the dances are accompanied only by effects on the drums.*

Oh, no, that's not strictly a jig. More of a Morris dance. Did you do that for long?

BOOT. **No, sir. Then I did this.** [*He does a complicated turn*]

INSPECTOR. **You actually did a left turn like that! Fascinating survival. There hasn't been anything like that since the Caucasian Fertility Rite. What did you do after that?** [*He moves down* LC]

BOOT. **This, sir.** [*He dances*]

INSPECTOR. **English Folk. Go on.**

BOOT *dances.*

You have done a complete figure from *Jenny Pluck Pears*. **Did you know that? Well, what did you do after that?**

BOOT *dances down* L.

Jig, jig, keelrow, jig, jig—*Swan Lake*. **It's good, you've got it in your feet, Boot. What were the others doing?**

BOOT *does some Rock and Roll.*

Teddy Boys' Picnic!

BOOT *dances a Russian dance.*

Un-American activities. Anything else?

BOOT. **I can't remember any more, sir.**

INSPECTOR. **Pity! Well, Boot, what seems to be the trouble?**

BOOT *is speechless.*

Did you question the pianist?

BOOT. **I was in no position, to, sir.**

INSPECTOR. **Why? What position . . . ?**

BOOT [*moving to* L *of the Inspector*] **I wish to resign from the Force, sir.**

INSPECTOR. **Now relax, Boot.**

BOOT [*removing his helmet; almost in tears*] **I'm a failure, sir.**

INSPECTOR [*moving to the gramophone*] **I shall come along with you myself.**

BOOT. **To make an arrest, sir?**

INSPECTOR. **Certainly not, Boot.** [*He takes a pair of ballet shoes from the gramophone cupboard*] **To join in.**   MUSIC

> The INSPECTOR *holds up the ballet shoes.* The LIGHTS *dime to* BLACK-OUT *as—*

> LIGHTING CUE 14

> *the* RUNNING TABS *close*

SCENE 8

The Park

The Scene commences in front of the RUNNING TABS.

> LIGHTING CUE 15

> *When the* LIGHTS *come up.* NIGEL *enters* L, *engrossed in a newspaper.* JANE *enters* R. *They pass each other, then* NIGEL *stops and turns.*

NIGEL. **Jane!**

JANE [*stopping and turning*] **Nigel!**

> *They meet* C *and embrace.*

I thought it was you.

NIGEL. **How are you? I haven't seen you all the summer. I've missed you.**

JANE. **I've been a bit busy for parties and things.**

NIGEL. **I am sorry. Your mother's asked me to your party.**

JANE. **I know.**

NIGEL. **Jolly good!** [*He moves close to her*] **I say, have you seen this?** [*He taps his paper*] **It's about the piano.**

JANE [*backing* LC] **Piano?**

NIGEL. **You know, the one that makes people dance in the parks. Surely you've heard of it?**

JANE. **Oh, yes. Vaguely.**

NIGEL [*moving to* R *of her*] **It sounds a frightfully good thing—**[*he pulls Jane to him*] **but listen to this.** [*He reads*] **"Panic in the parks. Minister bans playful piano."**

JANE [*crossing to* RC] **Bans!**

NIGEL. **Mm!** [*He reads*] **"The Minister of Pleasure and Pastime, Mr Augustine Williams, announced today that the peaceful seclusion of London's parks has lately been disrupted by an alarming outbreak of dancing. The cause of this ever-increasing epidemic is a certain street piano, played by a young man and a girl whose identity has not yet been discovered.**

JANE. **Thank goodness.**

NIGEL. **Mm? Yes, jolly good!** [*He reads*] **"In spite of frequent police intervention many Londoners have already danced to the piano, including one of the sentries at Buckingham Palace."**

> JANE *takes the paper and crosses to* LC.

JANE [*reading*] **"In view of these dangerous symptoms of mass hysteria, the Minister has ordered a search for the offending piano and its mystery owners." Well! All I can say is I hope they jolly well get away with it.**

NIGEL. **So do I. Minister of Pleasure and Pastime, indeed! All he ever does is to restrain pleasure—in other people, that is to say.**

JANE [*moving to* L *of Nigel*] **Why?** [*She hands him the paper*] **Has he a pleasure and pastime of his own?**

> NIGEL *glances round, then takes* JANE's *arm and leads her* RC.

NIGEL [*conspiratorially*] **You know the night club called** *The Cleopatra?*

JANE. **Yes.**

NIGEL. **Well, I've heard he goes there every night, and all because of Asphynxia.**

JANE. **A—what?**

NIGEL. **Asphynxia. Oh, she's a singer there.**

JANE [*excitedly*] **If we could prove that, he wouldn't have the face to ban Minnie—er—the piano.**

NIGEL. **Then why don't we go there tonight and catch him at it?**

JANE. **Oh, Nigel! I can't! I'm meeting someone.**

NIGEL. **What—here?**

JANE. **Yes. We're going to a piano recital.**

The RUNNING TABS *open*

FINALE

NIGEL. **Oh. Oh, well, I'd better push off, then.** [*He moves up* RC] **Cheerio, Jane.**

JANE. **Good-bye, Nigel.**

NIGEL [*pausing then moving* C] **We'll go blackmailing some other time.**

JANE. **That'll be fun. Good-bye.**

NIGEL *exits quickly* R. JANE *drifts to* R.

TIMOTHY *runs on up* L *and crosses to* L *of Jane.*

TIMOTHY. **Jane, it's all up. I've just been photographed with Minnie.**

JANE. **No!**

TIMOTHY. **Yes. The Press. Thank heavens mother takes** *The Times.* [*He moves* C]

JANE [*moving* RC] **Is Troppo bringing her?**

TIMOTHY. **Yes, in a minute.**

NIGEL *enters* R.

NIGEL [*moving to* R *of Jane*] **I say, Jane . . .** [*He sees Timothy*] **Oh, I'm sorry.**

JANE. **Timothy Dawes—Nigel Danvers.**

NIGEL [*down* R *of Jane*] **How do you do?**

TIMOTHY [*eagerly*] **How do you do?** [*He realizes*] **Who?**

JANE. **Nigel Danvers. Tim, you've heard me speak of him.**

TIMOTHY [*dashed*] **Yes, I have. How do you do?** [*He moves up* LC]

NIGEL. **Sorry to butt in like this. I only came back to see if you would care to come along to** *The Cleopatra after* **your engagement.**

TIMOTHY [*moving to* L *of Jane*] **Oh, you've met already this evening.**

JANE. **Tim!**

TIMOTHY. **I suppose you're one of the chaps going to Jane's mother's party.**

NIGEL. **Yes.**

TIMOTHY. **I thought so.**

JANE. **Tim, really!**

NIGEL. **I say, would you care to come along, too?**

TIMOTHY. **Sorry, I'm busy. I'm giving a piano recital.** [*He moves* C]

NIGEL. **Oh.**

JANE. **It isn't the same piano recital.**

TIMOTHY [*loudly*] **What** *are* **you talking about?**

JANE. **Tim, you're shouting.** [*To Nigel*] **It's about Minnie.**

NIGEL. **Minnie? Minnie who?**

JANE. **I'd better tell you everything. You're on our side already, anyway.**

TIMOTHY *moves to* L *of Jane.*

NIGEL [*quite mystified*] **I say—am I? Oh, jolly good!**

JANE [*aside to Timothy*] **I'd better take Nigel away and explain.**

NIGEL *drifts up* R.

TIMOTHY. **Why take him away?**

JANE. **It's easier that way, don't you think? Look, why don't you knock off early and meet** MUSIC
us at *The Cleopatra?*

TIMOTHY. **I wouldn't dream of butting in.**

JANE. **Oh, Tim, don't be stupid. You must realize how rude we've both been.**

TIMOTHY. **You didn't tell me you'd met him already this evening.**

JANE. **Why should I tell you everything?**

TIMOTHY. **Go with him, by all means. I suppose I can manage alone.**

JANE. **I should jolly well hope you can. I think you're being rather silly. Are you coming,
Nigel?**

JANE exits down R.

NIGEL. **M'm!** [*He moves down* R] **Well—we'll see you perhaps . . . ?**

TIMOTHY. **Good-bye.**

NIGEL. **Um—good-bye.**

NIGEL exits down R.

TIMOTHY. **Jane!**

TROPPO wheels the piano on L and sets the stool at it.

[*He runs and looks off down* R] **We weren't both rude—it was only me.** [*He turns and sees Troppo*] **Oh,
hullo, Troppo.**

TROPPO takes a packet of sandwiches from the piano.

[*He crosses to* LC] **Women provoke you and then turn on you.**

TROPPO moves to L of Timothy and offers him a sandwich.

Oh, no, I'm not hungry.

TROPPO mimes, inviting Timothy to play.

Yes, I know. [*He crosses and sits at the piano*] **She's not obliged to feel as I do. It wasn't part of
the agreement. Ready, Troppo?** [*He plays*]

DANCE, SONG AND DANCE No. 10

"OUT OF BREATH"

ENSEMBLE

TROPPO *dances.*

LIGHTING CUE 16

An AMERICAN *and a* SHOPGIRL *enter up* L *and dance lazily, without
surprise. The lamp in the park suddenly lights brilliantly. A* WELL-
DRESSED LADY, *two* THEATRE-GOERS *in evening dress and* ROWENA
enter and dance. NIGEL *and* JANE *enter and join in. Finally, and promi-
nently,* BOOT *and the* INSPECTOR *enter and are seen dancing together a
figure reminiscent of the office scene.*

ALL [*singing*] **Stop! Stop! We've had enough!**
Find the going far too rough.
Weary legs! Weary feet!
Nearly melting with the heat,
And *out,*
Completely *out of breath!*

Can't dance. Can't sing,
Can't do a single thing,
We're—so—out—of breath
Can't run. Can't walk.
Can't laugh or even talk,
We're—so—out—of breath.

Hold hard. Snatch a breath.
Ooh, ahh, catch a breath.
Heigh-ho, here's a shindy,
Puff, pant, windy, windy.

Can't move. Can't stand,
Must say the feeling's grand,
We're—so—out—of breath.

MEN. Can't dance. Can't sing.   GIRLS. Here where the
      Can't do a single thing.   London
      We're so out of breath   Lamps are bright
      Can't run. Can't walk.   Dancing and
      Can't laugh or even talk   Singing
      We're so out of breath   Through the night.

      Hold hard. Snatch a breath.   Here in the
      Ooh, aah, catch a breath   Heart of
      Heigh-ho, here's a shindy   London
      Puff, pant, windy, windy.   Town

      Can't move. Can't stand.   Dancing
      Must say the feeling's grand   Till we
      We're so out of breath.   All fall down.

DANCE

ALL. Quick, girls! Quick, boys!
      Let's make a final noise
      Though we're out of breath
      Here where the London lamps are bright,
      Dancing and singing through the night,
      Here in the heart of London Town
      Dancing till we all fall down.

      All fall down, all fall down, all fall down,
      All fall down, all fall down, all fall down,
      Dancing, dancing, dancing,
      Till we all fall down!

CURTAIN

ACT II

Scene 1

The Night Club

The backcloth depicts a scene of the desert, and c of it, there is a small curtained alcove with a stool in front of it. Wings R and L represent Egyptian temple pillars. There is an upright piano up R and a large gong on a stand up LC. Café tables and chairs stand down R, down L and up L. There are table-lamps, cloths and glasses, etc., on the tables. A stand microphone is beside the piano.

> *When the* CURTAIN *rises, the* RUNNING TABS *are closed, concealing the interior of the Club. In front of the* TABS, *there is a curtained door flat representing the exterior of "The Cleopatra". The name is written in lights above the doorway. There is a crash of cymbals.*

LIGHTING CUE 17

> *A spotlight focuses on the* MANAGER *as he bursts through the curtained doorway. He wears a fez and is heavily made-up as an Egyptian.*

SONG AND DANCE

No. 11

"CLEOPATRA"

MANAGER

MANAGER.   There was a lady of Egypt, I'm told,
The barge she sat on was of burnished gold,
Her moral code made the Sphinx perspire,
Her Roman Scandal set the Nile on fire.
They tried to make her marry her brother Ptolemy
She said, "I won't Ptolerate Ptolemy to collar me.
I only sell to the highest bids!"
Now she's hotting up the Pharoahs in the Pyramids.

Cleopatra.
Held the key to every heart-ra
And the secret of her art-ra
Was to keep her men at bay.
She used to tease her
Sugar-daddy Julius Caesar
By not allowing him to squeeze her
More than once or twice a day.

For when this minx was up to her jinks
She recalled the words of that wise old Sphinx
"Never let men become too chummy
Or you're sure to end up as an Egyptian mummy."

33

Cleopatra
Egypt's answer to Montmartra
Was so respectable a tart-ra
Her virtue almost seemed a crime.
And though more meaty
Than even luscious Neferteeti
She would reply to each entreaty
"Ptry calling back another p.ime."

The world it rang from Rome to Rio
With the affair of Anthony and Cleo,
And soothsayers swore that by the very next Ides
He'd be making her the first of the G.I. brides.
Now Tony's little kid-wife Octavia
Didn't quite appreciate this behaviour,
But Cleo acted like she didn't care
Till she went and shoved an asp-a down her you-know-where.

Cleopatra
Had forty lovers a la carte-ra
But number forty-one got smart-ra
He tried to wriggle free.
She smiled her smile and
She gently pushed him in the Nile and
She whistled up a crocodile and
Said, "Pompey darling, here's your ptea."
Her henna painted the whole town red.
Her nylons hit the Nile on the head,
But the only thing her men could wheedle
Was a nasty jab from Cleopatra's needle.

Cleopatra
Tore every other heart apart-ra
But she was truly in the cart-ra
When she went and lost her own.
Yes, that's the price, girls.
This love is very sweet and nice, girls,
But if you want a life of vice, girls,
Leave Mister Cupid well alone.
Take my advice, girls,
And never overload your dice, girls,
But keep your paramours on ice, girls,
And leave love alone.

The music continues as the door-flat is flown and the RUNNING TABS *open.*

LIGHTING CUE 18

The LIGHTS *come up on the interior of the nightclub. There are black* TABS
concealing the backcloth. The PIANIST *is seated at the piano, playing.* FIONA
is dancing desultorily with TOM SMITH. *The* MANAGER *moves up* R *and
leans on the piano. A* WAITRESS, *dressed as an Egyptian slave-girl, enters
down* L *carrying a tray with a bottle of champagne in a cooler. She crosses
and puts the tray on the piano. The music ceases.* FIONA *and* TOM *sit at the
table up* L. *The* SLAVE *enters through the* TABS *up* C. *He strikes an
Egyptian pose, looks at his wrist-watch, then strikes the gong. The black
TABS are flown revealing the* ARMS DANCERS.

LIGHTING CUE 19   MUSIC
Drum-beat

The LIGHTS *dim a little and a spotlight focuses on the* Dancers. *The* GIRL *sits on the stool in front of the backcloth, the* MAN *behind it, with his arms pushed through two slits in the cloth. The impression is of a four-armed dancer. The action is done rhythmically to a drum beat. The sequence of the dance is as follows.*

1. *Rhythmical movements to establish the absurdity of the arms.*

2. *The* GIRL *feels a sneeze coming on. Each hand in turn goes under her nose. Finally all hands together. She sneezes. The* MAN *takes a handchief from her bosom and wipes her nose. He puts the handkerchief back.*

3. *The* GIRL *takes out a cigarette. The* MAN *takes out matches and lights the cigarette. He hands the matches to the* SLAVE, *then takes the cigarette from the* GIRL's *mouth and she loses track of which hand it is in. She tries each in turn and finally nudges the hand that holds it. She takes a puff then hands the cigarette to the* SLAVE.

4. *The* MAN's *hands begin to become familiar. He tickles each of the* GIRL's *knees, and under the arms. She grows more and more alarmed. He strangles her.*

LIGHTING CUE 20

The LIGHTS BLACK-OUT.

The SLAVE *and the* ARMS DANCERS *exit in the* BLACK-OUT, *then the* LIGHTS *come up as at the beginning of the scene.*

LIGHTING CUE 21

JANE *and* NIGEL *enter up* L *and cross to* C. *The* PIANIST *plays softly.*

JANE. **You must have thought we were mad.**
NIGEL. **I just wondered who Minnie was.**

The MANAGER *moves to Jane and Nigel.*

MANAGER. **Good evening, Lord Danvers. This way, Lord Danvers. Miss Raeburn.** [*He conducts them to the table down* R]
JANE *sits above the table down* R. NIGEL *stands* L *of Jane.*
Champagne, Lord Danvers?
NIGEL. **Thank you.**

The MANAGER *moves up* R *and takes the champagne from the tray.*

JANE. **Is Gus Williams here yet?**
NIGEL [*looking around*] **Not yet.**

FIONA *laughs.*

JANE [*looking towards Fiona*] **Oh, there's a girl I know. In fact, she's an old friend of mine.**
FIONA [*to Nigel*] **Hullo.**
NIGEL. **Hullo.** [*To Fiona*] **I say, would you like them to join us?** [*He crosses and sits* R *of the table down* R]
JANE. **I think she's all right where she is.**

The MANAGER *moves to the table down* R *and pours champagne for Jane and Nigel. He listens too intently.*

You know, you're full of surprises, Nigel. You're really quite nice and disreputable.
NIGEL. **Oh, it's nothing.** [*To the Manager*] **Thank you.**

The MANAGER *moves up* R.

JANE. **I say, I wish he'd come.**
NIGEL. **He usually arrives just before Asphynxia does her act.**

AUGUSTINE WILLIAMS *enters up* L.

Sh! Here he comes now.
  JANE. **That's him!**

WILLIAMS crosses to C. The MANAGER crosses to R of Williams.

  NIGEL. **Look at him—the Minister of Pleasure and Pastime.**
  MANAGER. **Good evening, Mr Williams.** [*He conducts him to the table down* L] **This way, Mr Williams.**

The WAITRESS crosses to LC. WILLIAMS sits at the table down L, a figure of monumental weariness.

Your favourite dish, Mr Williams? [*To the Waitress*] **Charmian—two eggs and chips.**

The WAITRESS crosses and exits up R.

The MANAGER follows her off.

The GIRL DANCER enters up R.

  NIGEL. **A front page picture of him looking like that would settle my point right away.**
  JANE. **We mustn't be hasty, Nigel. Ask the pianist to play something a little livelier.**
  NIGEL [*rising*] **All right, but I don't suppose it will have any success.** [*He goes to the pianist, then crosses slowly up* C]

FIONA rises and crosses to Jane.

  FIONA. **Jane.** [*She sits* R *of the table down* R]
  JANE. **Hello, Fiona.**
  FIONA. **Quick, before he comes back—tell me who your heavenly man is.**
  JANE. **Nigel Danvers.**

NIGEL talks to TOM, who rises.

  FIONA. **He is, without exception, the most marvellous thing I've ever seen in the whole of my life.**
  JANE. **Who's your friend?**
  FIONA. **Oh, my dear, it's too shame-making. I met him at the Plunketts' garden party and made a date with him before I** *knew*.
  JANE. **Knew?**
  FIONA. **He wasn't a guest at all—he was a press photographer.**
  JANE. **That's very convenient.**

NIGEL and TOM move slowly to L of the table down R. NIGEL is R of Tom.

  FIONA. **My dear, I think it is, without exception, the** *fauxest pas* **I have ever made in the whole of my life.**
  JANE. **Here's Nigel.**

The DANCER sits at the table up L.

  FIONA. **Oh.** [*She turns away in a flutter of expectation*]
  JANE. **Nigel, I want you to meet an old school friend of mine. Fiona Thompson. Fiona . . .**

FIONA gazes out front.

[*Loudly*] **Fiona.**
  FIONA [*turning with an innocent air of surprise*] **Mmm?**
  JANE. **Do you know Nigel Danvers?**
  FIONA. **Why no, I don't believe I do.**
  NIGEL. **How do you do?**
  FIONA. **Lord Danvers—Tom Smith.**

The MANAGER enters up R, moves up C and gives the Dancer a dirty look.

The DANCER rises.

  JANE. **Nigel, Tom's a press photographer.**

NIGEL. **Yes, I know. We've just been talking to each other—Tom's going to help.**   <ins>MUSIC</ins>

FIONA. **Help what?**

NIGEL. **He's got his camera here and he's going to take a picture of you-know-who.**

The DANCER *exits up* R.

FIONA. **But I don't know who. Who?**

The MANAGER *tidies the table and chairs up* L.

JANE. **The dreary old thing over there.**

NIGEL. **Augustine Williams.**

JANE. **We want a picture of him dancing with Asphynxia.**

NIGEL. **Or anybody. We just want him to let himself go.**

FIONA. **Oh, do let me try. I'm awfully good at making people let themselves go.**

JANE. **Would you really, Fiona?**

NIGEL. **And let Tom take a picture?**

FIONA [*rising*] **Darling, I don't understand a thing that's going on, but I'm crazy to join in.**

JANE. **Well, hurry up, because Asphynxia's due on any minute.**

FIONA *crosses to* R *of Williams.* TOM *collects his camera from the table up* L.

FIONA [*perching on the table down* L] **Mr Williams, I must tell you how much I enjoyed your speech in the House yesterday.** [*She tweaks Williams' ear*] **It was wonderful, and so long. I was in the Visitors' Gallery. I couldn't get a seat in the stalls. I simply adore the Commons, they're so much more exhilarating than the Lords, don't you think?**

REPRISE   No. 11a

[*Over the music*] **Listen to this music. Doesn't it do things to you? Dance, Mr Williams? Dance? You know, dancing's awfully good for the constitution. I know I'm silly but this sort of music simply knocks me out.**

FIONA *pulls* WILLIAMS *to his feet and they dance Spanish style.* TOM *takes a photograph of them.*

The WAITRESS *enters up* R *with a plate of egg and chips on a tray and crosses to Fiona and Williams.*

The SLAVE *enters up* L.

WAITRESS. **Two eggs and chips.**

WILLIAMS *takes the plate of eggs and chips, returns to the table down* L *and sits.* FIONA, *disappointed, returns to her seat at the table down* R.

The WAITRESS *exits up* R. *The* PIANIST *rises, sets a microphone* C, *then returns to his seat. The* SLAVE *strikes the gong.*

SONG   No. 12

"SAND IN MY EYES"

ASPHYNXIA

ASPHYNXIA *enters up* R *and moves to the microphone* C.

ASPHYNXIA.
    I walk through a desert
    A desert of love.
    And I stand—gosh, how I stand
    On the hot Egyptian sand.
    And I blink at those blinding skies
    For you are the sand in my eyes.

You're so catchable
And so unmatchable
And, darling, you're semi-detachable
You're the sand in my eyes.
[*She coughs into the microphone*]
You're so beautiful
So undutiful
And, sweetheart, you're so tutti-fruttiful
You're the sand in my eyes.

Kiss me, kiss me, kiss me, kiss me,
Hold me close to you.
Shatter me, batter me, break my anatomy
Prove your love is true.

Oh, you're so mystical
Egotistical
And sub-existentialistical
You're the sand in my eyes.

MUSIC

LIGHTING CUE 22

The LIGHTS BLACK-OUT *as*—

the RUNNING TABS *close*

SCENE 2

Night Frontcloth

The scene is played in front of the RUNNING TABS.

LIGHTING CUE 23

When the LIGHTS *come up,* TIMOTHY *wheels the piano on* R. JANE *and*
NIGEL *enter* L.

JANE [*crossing to* LC] **Would you say she was a pleasure or a pastime?**

TIMOTHY *sets the piano* C *and tries to back off* R, *unnoticed.*

NIGEL [*moving to* L *of Jane*] **Perhaps he just likes her voice.**

JANE *crosses to* C *and sees Timothy.*

JANE. **Tim.**
TIMOTHY [*stopping*] **Oh, hullo.**
JANE. **You haven't been playing till now?**
TIMOTHY. **No, I was just taking a stroll.**
JANE. **We had a gorgeous time at** *The Cleopatra.* [*She stands in front of the piano*]

TIMOTHY *stands* R *of the piano,* NIGEL *stands* L *of it.*

TIMOTHY. **Oh, good!**
JANE. **We tried to hatch a plot.**
NIGEL. **But it didn't work. He had no film in the camera.**
JANE. **It was an awfully good plot, though. You know the Minister of Pleasure and Pastime . . . ?**
TIMOTHY. **Very well—he's my uncle.**

MUSIC

NIGEL. **What?**

TIMOTHY. **I told you I had an uncle in the Cabinet.**

JANE. **Yes, but I thought you were just pulling my leg.**

TIMOTHY. **I don't know why my uncles are always funny to you.**

NIGEL. **I say, I am terribly sorry. We'll call off the campaign right away.**

TIMOTHY. **That's all right. I don't like him very much, anyway.**

JANE. **It was stuffy in that place.**

NIGEL. **Yes, it was.** [*He puts an arm around Jane's waist*] **It's just nice now.** [*He looks up*] **I say, look, there's the Plough.**

JANE. **Yes.**

NIGEL. **And the Milky Way.**

JANE [*disbelieving*] **No!**

NIGEL. **Honestly.**

There is a pause.

TIMOTHY. **I've got to go and see him on Wednesday.**

JANE. **Who, darling?**

TIMOTHY. **Uncle Augustine.**

JANE. **Oh.**

There is a pause.

NIGEL. **Jane.**

JANE. **Yes?**

NIGEL. **Do you manage Minnie alone?**

JANE. **No.**

NIGEL. **Would you like to come out with me next Wednesday night?**

JANE *hesitates.*

TIMOTHY. **Why not?**

JANE. **Mm?**

NIGEL. **Why not?**

JANE. **Mm. Nigel, there's something we haven't told you.**

NIGEL. **Apart from Minnie?**

JANE. **Apart from Minnie. Tim and I are married, Nigel.**

NIGEL *moves quickly* LC.

NIGEL [*after a pause*] **Since when?**

JANE [*to Timothy*] **Since when?**

TIMOTHY. **Three weeks and a day.**

There is a pause.

NIGEL. **This** *is* **a surprise.**

JANE. **Worse than Minnie?**

NIGEL. **Well, Minnie was** *nice.*

JANE [*tenderly*] **Oh, Nigel!**

TIMOTHY [*flatly*] **It doesn't** *matter,* **though.**

JANE [*to Nigel*] **We mean, I could still go out with you, only I'd say "yes" in a different way.**

NIGEL. **I see. Yes, I do see.**

TIMOTHY. **We could cancel it, if necessary.**

JANE. **What?**

TIMOTHY [*moving* RC] **The marriage, I mean.**

JANE. **No, we couldn't, Tim. Don't confuse, Nigel, he's anxious enough about his campaign.**

TIMOTHY. **We said at the first it was only for convenience.**

JANE [*explanatory, to Nigel*] **Yes. But that we might fall in love,** *after.*

NIGEL. **I see.**

JANE. **And that we wouldn't mind it being permanent if it turned out that way.**

NIGEL. **And it has turned out that way.**

JANE. Oh, yes. Once we were married, we lost no time in falling in love.
NIGEL [*moving* L] Oh, well. That's nice. I hate long engagements.

There is a pause.

TIMOTHY [*moving to Jane*] I don't quite understand. Did we mean all that last bit? Or are we just comforting Nigel?
JANE. You are silly. It *doesn't* comfort Nigel. It only makes things clear.
TIMOTHY. Jane! [*He embraces her*]
NIGEL. Perhaps I could marry Minnie.

TIMOTHY *suddenly comes to life and crosses eagerly to* R *of Nigel.*

TIMOTHY. You can *have* Minnie, if you like.
JANE. Tim!
TIMOTHY [*moving to* L *of Jane*] No, I didn't mean that, of course. [*To Nigel*] I mean, what will you have—er—what would you like?

NIGEL *moves slowly to* L *of Timothy.*

I mean, I'd like to *give* you something, if possible.
NIGEL. That's all right. Jolly good—congratulations.
TIMOTHY. Oh, thanks. I know what—we can help Nigel in his campaign against Uncle Augustine.
JANE. Yes, Tim.
NIGEL. That would be wonderful.
TIMOTHY. Oh, good! Well—[*he crosses to* RC] what shall we do now? It's too soon to go home. Are you tired?
JANE. No.
TIMOTHY. Are you, Nigel?
NIGEL. No.
TIMOTHY. Then let's sing.
JANE. Yes, let's sing.
NIGEL. Why sing, exactly?
JANE. Because it's the middle of the night.
TIMOTHY. It's nearly morning.
JANE. Because it's nearly morning.
NIGEL. I can't sing.
JANE [*moving to* R *of Nigel*] Now, Nigel.
NIGEL. No, honestly. I'm not being funny. I never could.
TIMOTHY. Anyone can.
NIGEL. No, honestly. Even in church my sisters used to nudge me to shut up.

TIMOTHY *and* JANE *laugh.*

JANE [*moving* C] Try.
TIMOTHY. It's easy.

TRIO

"IT'S EASY TO SING"

No. 13

JANE, TIMOTHY *and* NIGEL

JANE.

Tap the rhythm with your feet,
Try to keep a steady beat,
Follow me and then repeat,
You can't go very far wrong.

MUSIC

TIMOTHY.	**Not too quick and not too slow,**
	Not too high and not too low
JANE *and* TIMOTHY.	**Ready, steady, off you go**
	And snap—you're singing my song.

TIMOTHY and NIGEL lift JANE on to the top of the piano.

JANE.	**It's easy to sing a simple song,**
	If you sing it after me.
	It's easy to sing a simple song
	As it is to climb a tree.
	It's easy to catch a simple snatch
	Of a tuneful melody.
	It's easy to sing a simple song
	If you sing it after me.

JANE *and* TIMOTHY.	**Sing, sing, sing,**
	Sing it after me.
	Sing, sing, sing,
	Sing it after me.

JANE [*spoken*] **Nigel, you see if you can do it.**
NIGEL. **Do you think I will be able to remember it?**
JANE. **Of course you will.** [*She sings*]

	La–la–la–la–la.
NIGEL [*singing*]	**It's easy to sing**
JANE.	**La—la—la—la**
NIGEL [*off key*]	**A simple song**
JANE. **La—la—la—la—la—la—la**	

NIGEL.	**If I sing it after you.**
	It's easy to sing a simple song,
	As it is to tie a shoe.
	It's easy to pick the tune up quick
	And to hum it gaily through.
	It's easy to sing a simple song
	If I sing it after you.

ALL.	**Sing, sing, sing,**
NIGEL.	**Sing it after you.**
ALL.	**Sing, sing, sing**
NIGEL.	**Sing it after you.**

ALL.	**It's easy to sing a simple song,**
	If you sing it after us.
	It's easy to sing a simple song
	As it is to board a bus.
	It's easy to tell, we all sing well,
	When we sing without a fuss.
	It's easy to sing a simple song
	If you sing it after us.

	Sing, sing, sing,
	Sing it after us.
	Sing, sing, sing,

MUSIC

Sing it after us.
Sing, sing, sing,
Sing it after us.

They wheel the piano slowly off R.

Sing it after us,
Sing it after us.

Their voices fade into the distance as—

the LIGHTS BLACK-OUT   LIGHTING CUE 24

SCENE 3

The Park Café Terrace

There is a café table RC, *with chairs* R *and* L *of it.*

LIGHTING CUE 25

When the RUNNING TABS *open, the* LIGHTS *come up.* TROPPO *is seated*
R *of the table, reading a comic paper and drinking an ice-cream soda.* BOOT
enters up L, *crosses and looks over Troppo's shoulder at the comic.* TROPPO
turns away, but finally gives the comic to BOOT *who sits* L *of the table.*
BOOT *looks at the ice-cream soda.* TROPPO *hesitates then gives* BOOT *a*
straw and they both drink simultaneously from the glass. WILLIAMS *enters*
up L *and crosses to Boot.*

WILLIAMS. **Boot!**

BOOT *rises and stands to attention.*

Have you located the piano yet, Boot?
  BOOT. **Not yet, sir.**
  WILLIAMS. **It is fast becoming a national problem. We must on no account allow ourselves**
to take a flippant view of the situation. [*He takes the comic from Boot*] **I have already spent hours**
in conference with . . . [*He reads the comic*] **"Bill and Ben, the flowerpot men." The piano must**
be suppressed. It is a threat to our dignity. Do not think for one moment that it would
have any effect on me . . . [*He reads*] **". . . but I think I shall eat a turnip to make my tummy**
feel brave."

BOOT *crosses above Williams to* L *of him.* TROPPO *rises and crosses to*
R *of Williams.*

As I was doing my rounds this morning . . . [*He reads*] **". . . lots of little teardrops were plop-**
ping off the willow trees into the pond, plop, plop, plop——

TROPPO *turns the page for Williams.*

—plop." The Prime Minister was seriously disturbed. [*He reads*] **"Dear me," he said,**
"whatever will little Dumpling think?" So, Boot, we will lie in wait for these renegades,
conceal ourselves behind the bushes . . . [*He reads*] **". . . and wait until next Monday for a**
further adventure with Woppit." I'll stick to *Reveille.* (*He returns the comic to Boot.*)

BOOT *and* WILLIAMS *exit up* L. TROPPO *sits* R *of the table.*

TIMOTHY *enters up* R, *carrying a bathing towel and his shoes and socks.*

TIMOTHY [*sitting* L *of the table*] **Gosh, it was cold in.** [*He puts on his shoes and socks*] **You were very**
wise not to come, Troppo. I say, for a horrible moment I thought I saw you with Uncle
Augustine.

TROPPO *pulls a face.*

Have you seen Jane? She said she was meeting Fiona here. We'll have to manage Minnie MUSIC
alone this afternoon. Jane's got to go to Gusset Creations to try to buy herself a new party
frock. [*He reads the comic*]

TROPPO takes the comic, tears it in half and gives half to Timothy.

JANE enters up L and moves to L of Timothy.

JANE. **Hullo.**

TROPPO rises and exits R. TIMOTHY rises and casually kisses Jane.

TIMOTHY. **Hullo, darling.** [*He resumes his seat*]

JANE crosses and sits R of the table.

When are you going to Gusset Creations?
JANE. **Soon. I've asked Fiona to meet me here.**
TIMOTHY. **Fiona?**
JANE. **Yes, you remember.**
TIMOTHY. **Oh, yes, of course.**
JANE. **Where's Minnie?**

TROPPO enters R with an ice-cream soda which he puts on the table in front of Jane.

TIMOTHY. **Still in the garage. Come along, Troppo, we'll go and get her out.** [*To Jane*] **Will
you still be here when we come back?**

TROPPO picks up the comic and moves down R.

JANE. **Yes, I think so. Hurry up.**

TIMOTHY crosses to LC. TROPPO pockets the comic and follows Timothy.

FIONA enters up R.

TIMOTHY. **Hullo.**
FIONA. **Oh, hullo.**
TIMOTHY. **We're going to get Minnie.** [*To Jane*] **'Bye, darling.** [*To Fiona*] **'Bye.**
JANE. **'Bye.**
TIMOTHY. **Troppo!**

TIMOTHY exits L.

TROPPO doffs his cap to Fiona and follows Timothy off.

FIONA [*moving to L of the table RC*] **Minnie who? Darling, what *is* going on? It all sounds abso-
lutely thrilling, but I don't understand a word.**
JANE [*indicating her drink*] **Will you have one of these?**
FIONA. **No, darling, I hate them. They're so wind-making.** [*She moves C*] **Who was that who
said hullo to me just now?**
JANE. **Timothy.**
FIONA. **Who's Timothy?**
JANE. **Fiona, can you keep a secret?**

FIONA runs to the chair L of the table and sits.

FIONA. **Of course I can, darling—you know I can. I'm as safe as a tomb.**
JANE. **Well, that young man you met just now—he's my husband.**
FIONA. **Your . . . ? Oh, my poor darling!**
JANE. **No, no. You don't understand. I *wanted* to marry him. Only please don't tell anybody
just yet, Fiona.**
FIONA. **I promise. I really do promise. And what about Nigel?**
JANE. **Oh, he's just a friend.**
FIONA. **That is, without exception, the most marvellous thing I have heard in the whole
of my life.**
JANE [*looking at her watch*] **I must go.** [*She rises*] **I'm just off to Gusset Creations to buy a new**

dress for my party on the tenth. Mother's arranged a dress parade specially. Do come and   MUSIC
help me choose. [*She moves down* R]

FIONA [*rising and moving to* L *of Jane*] I'd adore to. Everyone says I've got wonderful taste in
other people's clothes.

NIGEL *is heard off* L *singing "It's Easy to Sing"*.

JANE. It must be. It's Nigel!

NIGEL *enters up* L.

FIONA [*with a step towards him*] Hullo, Nigel.
NIGEL [*moving* C] Hullo, Fiona.
FIONA [*moving to* L *of the table*] Do tell me, what was that tune you were singing just then?
NIGEL [*moving* LC] Well, I suppose you might call it my signature tune.
FIONA [*moving* C] It was, without exception, the most beautiful thing I have ever heard in
the whole of my life.
NIGEL. Actually—Jane taught it to me.
FIONA. Then you must teach it to me.
JANE [*moving* RC] Yes, but do it as we go along or we shall be late.
NIGEL [*crossing to* L *of Jane*] Late for what?
JANE. The dress parade. You're going to help me choose a dress, Nigel.
NIGEL [*doubtfully*] Oh, jolly good.
FIONA [*moving to* L *of Nigel*] Come along, Nigel. How do we start?

REPRISE   No. 13a

"IT'S EASY TO SING"

JANE, FIONA *and* NIGEL

JANE *and* NIGEL.	Tap the rhythm with your feet,
	Try to keep a steady beat.
	Follow me, and then repeat,
	You can't go very far wrong.
	Not too quick and not too slow
FIONA.	Not too high and not too low.
JANE *and* NIGEL.	Ready, steady, off you go
	And snap—you're singing my song.
	It's easy to sing a simple song
	If you sing it after us.
	It's easy to sing a simple song
	As it is to board a bus.
FIONA.	It's easy to tell, we all sing well
	When we sing without a fuss
ALL.	It's easy to sing a simple song
	If you sing it after us.
	Sing, sing, sing,
	Sing it after us,
	Sing, sing, sing,
	Sing it after us.

TIMOTHY *and* TROPPO *wheel the piano on up* R *and set it* LC *with the shafts
facing* R.

NIGEL. Oh, hullo.
TIMOTHY. Hullo.

MUSIC

JANE. **This is Timothy, Fiona.**
FIONA [*moving to* R *of Timothy; doubtfully*] **How do you do?**
TIMOTHY. **How d'you do?**
JANE. **And this is Troppo.**
FIONA [*shaking hands with Troppo; more doubtfully*] **How do you do?**
TIMOTHY [*looking off* R] **My goodness! Look! There's Uncle Augustine.**
JANE. **What?**
TIMOTHY. **Jane! He mustn't see Minnie. Hide her.**
NIGEL. **Quick. In front of the piano—Fiona.**

> *They stand in a row concealing the piano.* TIMOTHY *is* R, JANE *is* L *of Timothy,* FIONA *is* L *of Jane and* NIGEL *is* L *of Fiona.* TROPPO *stands* R *of the piano.*

FIONA [*plaintively*] **I don't understand a single thing that's happening.**
NIGEL. **I'll explain later.**
FIONA. **Yes, when we're alone.**
TIMOTHY. **Troppo, as soon as you can, get Minnie back to where we were yesterday.**

> TROPPO *nods vigorously.*

Hide her well until I come.

> TROPPO *nods.*

> WILLIAMS *enters* R.

WILLIAMS. **Well, Timothy.** [*He holds out his hand*]
TIMOTHY. **Hello, Uncle Augustine.**

> *In order to shake hands, the whole group moves with Timothy.*

WILLIAMS. **Are these friends of yours?**

> TROPPO *panics. The group moves back to the piano.*

TIMOTHY. **Yes—no—we were just——**

> TROPPO, *concealed by Nigel, Jane and Fiona, wheels the piano off* L.

—passing the—er—time of day. [*He moves* C] **I was coming to see you on Wednesday.**
WILLIAMS [*crossing to* R *of Timothy*] **So you were. I'm glad I ran into you, Timothy. You might be able to help me.**
TIMOTHY [*guardedly*] **Help you?**
WILLIAMS [*crossing below Timothy and Jane to* R *of Fiona*] **And something tells me that your friends might be able to help me also.**
JANE [*moving to* L *of Timothy; aside*] **Oh, dear—he's recognized us.**
WILLIAMS. **The fact is, I'm looking for a piano.**

> *They all start guiltily.*

FIONA [*moving towards Williams*] **Oh, I know where there's one . . .**
NIGEL [*interrupting quickly*] **Just any old piano, sir?**
WILLIAMS. **No, no. The one people dance to in the park.** [*He fixes his eye on Nigel*] **Perhaps you can tell me who owns it?**
NIGEL. **Er—are you talking to me, sir?**
WILLIAMS. **Yes, young man, I am. Do I detect a "rebellious" tone in your voice?**
JANE [*whispering*] **He knows who we are, Tim.**
WILLIAMS [*turning to Jane*] **Ha! Perhaps** *you* **can help me. Have you ever seen this notorious instrument?**
JANE [*gaily*] **It's no use asking me. I don't go about much.**
WILLIAMS. **Not even to night clubs? What do you do with yourself, then?**

MUSIC

JANE [*singing*] **I sit in the sun . . .**
TIMOTHY. **Ssh! Jane—not now.**
WILLIAMS [*turning to Fiona*] **And this young lady. When did you last see the piano?**
FIONA [*innocently*] **I saw it a moment ago.**
NIGEL. **Oh, Fiona!**
WILLIAMS. **Aha!** [*He crosses to* RC, *waving his umbrella and calling*] **Boot!**

The others group LC.

JANE. **Fiona, you've given the whole game away.**
FIONA. **I didn't know it was a** *game*.

Boot enters down R. TIMOTHY *puts on dark glasses*.

WILLIAMS. **Any sign of the piano, Boot?**
BOOT [*moving to* R *of Williams*] **No, sir.**
WILLIAMS [*looking at Nigel*] **Any sign of the owners, Boot?**
BOOT [*moving down* R] **Just a glimpse, sir.**
WILLIAMS. **Well?**
BOOT [*pointing to Timothy*] **Him, sir.** [*He points to Jane*] **And her, sir.**
WILLIAMS. **What! Is this true, Timothy?**
TIMOTHY. **Yes, sir.** [*He removes the glasses*]
BOOT [*crossing to* R *of Timothy; triumphantly*] **I arrest you in the name of the . . .**
WILLIAMS [*moving down* R] **Now, just a moment, Boot. Don't be so impulsive. We can't arrest them without the piano.**
BOOT [*crossing to Williams*] **We can't arrest them** *with* **the piano, sir.**
WILLIAMS. **Why not?**
BOOT. **We'd be in no position to, sir.**
WILLIAMS [*crossing below Boot to* R *of Timothy*] **Timothy, where is it?**
TIMOTHY. **I've lost it.**
WILLIAMS. **Well, then, we must all help each other to find it, mustn't we?**
TIMOTHY. **So that I can be arrested, sir?**
WILLIAMS. **Nephew, it is your duty as an Englishman to co-operate. This is a matter of national importance.**
NIGEL [*darkly*] **I'll bet it is.** [*Aside to Fiona*] **The old So-and-so.**
WILLIAMS [*shaking his umbrella at Boot*] **Boot—**[*he crosses down* R] **it is your personal responsibility to find the piano.**
BOOT. **But, sir . . .**
TIMOTHY [*moving to* L *of Boot*] **I'm beginning to help, but it's difficult to know how to begin.**

Boot moves to L *of Williams*.

JANE [*moving to* L *of Timothy*] **We can always ask a policeman.**

NIGEL *and* FIONA *move* C.

TIMOTHY. **But, of course.** [*He moves to* L *of Boot. Charmingly*] **Excuse me, Constable—have you by any chance . . . ?**
BOOT. **Gertcha!**

CONCERTED NUMBER

"WE'RE LOOKING FOR A PIANO"

ENSEMBLE

Two PRESSMEN *enter up* C *during the introduction and come down* C. *The others turn and face them.*

PRESSMEN.	**We're looking for a piano.**
OTHERS.	**A piano?**
PRESSMEN.	**Yes, a piano.**
OTHERS.	**Just any old pia . . . ?**
PRESSMEN.	**No! The one that's rather rare.**
	We'll write in florid phrases
	Till its reputation blazes
	[They move L]
	From the page reserved for crazes

THREE RESPECTABLE LADIES *enter up* R.

In the tupp'ny *Daily Scare.*

The LADIES *come down* C.

LADIES.	**We're looking, we're looking,**
	We're look, look, look, look, looking,
	We're looking for a P-I-A-N-O,
	We're looking for a piano.
OTHERS.	**A piano?**
LADIES.	**Yes, a piano.**
OTHERS.	**Just any old pia . . . ?**
LADIES.	**No! The one that makes you dance.**
	Oh, are its methods drastic?
	We are so enthusiastic,
	When we tread the light fantastic,
	But we rarely get the chance.
TIMOTHY *and* JANE.	**It must be near to where we are.**
NIGEL *and* FIONA.	**We've seen it very lately,**
LADIES.	**You need not fear we'll go too far,**
	We only dance sedately.
BOOT *and* WILLIAMS.	**It's come, it's gone, it's out of sight**
	This piano's quite elusive.
PRESSMEN.	**We'd like to buy the rights to write,**
	And keep them quite exclusive.
ALL.	**We're looking, we're looking,**
	We're look, look, look, look, looking,
	We're looking for a P-I-A-N-O.
BOOT *and* WILLIAMS.	**We're looking for a piano.**
OTHERS.	**A piano?**
BOOT *and* WILLIAMS.	**Yes, a piano.**
OTHERS.	**Just any old pia . . . ?**

BOOT *and* WILLIAMS.

No! The one that's not allowed
It's owners are requested
To appear and be arrested,
For it makes the park congested
When they draw so large a crowd.

JANE *and* TIMOTHY.
FIONA *and* NIGEL.

They may decide to be benign,
But first it would be wise to
Be sure they're able to define
The crime they close their eyes to.

ALL.

Unlicensed joys are out of date,
They have to be recorded
On printed forms in triplicate
And filed away and hoarded.

We're looking, we're looking,
We're look, look, look, look, **looking,**
We're looking for a P-I-A-N-O.
We're looking for a piano
A piano? Yes, a piano.
Not any old pia . . . ?

No! The one that makes you gay.
We have a sort of notion
That a dash of sprightly **motion**
Is a stimulating potion
To be taken twice a day.
We're look, look, look, look, look, look,
Look, look, look, look, look, look,
Look, look, look, look, look, look,
Look, look, looking for a P-I-A-N-O
We're look, look, look, look, look, **look,**
Look, look, look, look, look, look,
Look, look, look, look, look, look,
Look, look, looking for a P-I-A-N-O
We're looking, we're looking,
We're look, look, look, look, looking,
We're looking for a P-I-A-N-O
Piano, piano, piano.

TIMOTHY, JANE, NIGEL *and* FIONA *come forward as—*

the RUNNING TABS *close behind them*

Scene 4

Frontcloth

The scene is played in front of the Tabs.

Jane, Fiona *and* Nigel *exit* r. Timothy *waves and turns to go.* Troppo *enters* l *in great distress.*

Timothy. **Hullo, Troppo. I was just coming to find you.**

Troppo show his distress.

What's the matter? Where's Minnie?

Troppo shrugs desperately.

Did you take her back to the garage?

Troppo shakes his head.

You haven't *left* her, Troppo? That's just what they want. To find *her* without us.

Troppo covers his face with his hands then mimes someone desperately looking for something.

Yes, they *are* looking for her.

Troppo shakes his head, points to Timothy and himself and searches again.

Oh, I see. [*He crosses to Troppo*] Look, Troppo. You thought I'd really lost her. Listen, I was just only pretending, then I said I'd help to find her just to lead them on—it was a *joke*, Troppo. [*He shakes Troppo*] Don't you understand, it was a joke. [*He breaks off*] No, wait a minute, what am I talking about? You *had* her. Of course, *you*.

They gaze at each other a moment.

Troppo, you don't mean you've really lost her?

Troppo hides his face.

But—but you had her just a moment ago. Now look, I'm not angry. You can tell me. Troppo, what happened?

Troppo mimes pushing the piano.

You were pushing Minnie—where?

Troppo makes swimming motions, then serpentine ones.

By the Serpentine—yes, go on.

Troppo mimes putting the piano down, walks a few steps down l, *turns does a double-take and throws up his hands in horror.*

You left her for a moment and she'd gone? But why did you leave her?

Troppo hangs his head.

Did you *have* to leave her?

Troppo nods energetically.

Was it something you wanted to do very badly?

Troppo nods.

Poor Troppo! Don't look like that. It wasn't your fault and we'll find her. But tell me, was there anyone you suspected?

Troppo nods and mimes children.

Children. Yes, could be. Some sort of game, I suppose. Well, Troppo, we've got to search MUSIC every inch. But, first we must go to Gusset Creations and get Jane. Come along, and keep your eyes skinned on the way.

REPRISE

No. 14a

"WE'RE LOOKING FOR A PIANO"

The music is played slowly and sadly.

TIMOTHY and TROPPO, *peering around, exit* L. *The music continues at a faster tempo.*

SCENE 5

The Dress Shop

The setting is in black drapes with a wide entrance up C. *There is an armchair* RC *and a sofa* LC. *Tall stands with vases of flowers are up* RC *and up* LC.

LIGHTING CUE 26

When the RUNNING TABS *open, the* LIGHTS *come up.* AMBROSE *enters up* C, *dancing to the music. He dusts the furniture and decorations extravagantly with a feather duster.* JANE, NIGEL *and* FIONA *enter down* R. *The music ceases.*

JANE [*moving below the armchair* RC] **Good afternoon, Ambrose.**
AMBROSE [*moving to* L *of Jane*] **Ah! Miss Raeburn.** [*He kisses her hand and draws her* C] **Good afternoon. How's your mum?**

FIONA *and* NIGEL *remain* RC. JANE *crosses below Ambrose and stands up* R *of the sofa.*

JANE. **I've come about my dress for my party on the tenth.**
AMBROSE. **Oh, Miss Raeburn, I have the most beautiful dress for you. It's so "*you*" it isn't true.**
JANE. **How lovely.** [*She sits on the sofa at the upstage end*] **Can I see it, please?**
AMBROSE. **Not yet. We must create the right atmosphere first.**

FIONA *crosses to* C.

JANE. **I hope it doesn't take too long. I have to get back to my work.**
FIONA. **Oh, Jane, you must see the dress parade.**

AMBROSE *turns to Fiona.*

It's sure to be heaven.
AMBROSE [*patting Fiona's head*] **Ah, children. I adore kiddies.** [*He sits Fiona on the downstage end of the sofa*] **Now, sit down there, dear, and don't make a noise.** [*He gets some books and sweets from the stand up* RC *and gives them to Fiona*] **Here's a couple of** *Beatrix Potters,* **and a bag of jelly babies.** [*He crosses to* L *of Nigel and curtsies*] **Oh, Lord Danvers—how's your mother, the dowager?**

NIGEL *crosses to* L *of the sofa and perches on the back of it.*

Did she ever get into that dress? She's one of my biggest customers. [*He snatches a scent spray from the stand up* RC *and douches the room with it*] **Ah, scent—delicious.** [*He moves to Jane*] **Try some.** [*He sprays Jane*] **Honeysuckle.**
FIONA. **Me, too.**
AMBROSE [*spraying Fiona*] **"You are my honey, honeysuckle—I am the bee."** [*He replaces the spray and moves up* C] **Now calm down, ladies and gentlemen, and prepare yourselves for a deep emotional experience.**

FIONA. **Does this mean we're going to see his Summer Collection?**
JANE. **I think so.**
AMBROSE. **Sh! Sh!** [*He claps his hands*]

> ROWENA *enters up* C *to announce the items. She is nervous and reads flatly and expressionlessly.*

ROWENA. **Do I start now, Mr Gusset?**
AMBROSE [*recoiling*] **My God, you look like a Canterbury Bell.**

> ROWENNA *moves below the armchair* RC.

[*He recovers and crosses to* L *of Rowena*] **Oh, this is Rowena. Don't be shy, Rowena.** [*To the others*] **Rowena's only just joined us and she's deputizing for Florence, who, as you know, Miss Raeburn, usually announces my collections.**
JANE. **I'm sure Rowena will do it very well.**

> ROWENA *leans forward and smiles at Jane.*

ROWENA. **Now?**
AMBROSE. **Yes.** [*He moves down* R]
ROWENA [*reading in the best Mayfair drawl she can muster*] **"Ladies and gentlemen, we have pleasure in presenting our Summer Collection. First, for casual outdoor wear, here is Marguerite to demonstrate an unusual and inexpensive model. You will find it very useful about the garden. We call it "Weedkiller".**

> MARGUERITE *enters up* C *to music played off. She demonstrates her exaggerated costume in the approved model style.* AMBROSE *crosses up* L, *straightening Marguerite's skirt as he passes, then stands above the sofa.*

"Note the complete freedom at the hips, and the fashionable body line. Your girl friends will be delighted by the rakish attitude of your father—your feather." **Oh, Mr Gusset, your writing!** **"Note the apronette so handy for your secateurs."**
NIGEL. **How do girls get themselves that shape?**
FIONA. **I couldn't possibly tell you until we know each other much better.**
ROWENA. **"Note the moulding of the bodice which gives the creation that tasteless look— that waistless look."** **Sorry, Mr Gusset.** **"Weedkiller comes in various sizes and can always be guaranteed to give you and your friends a perfect** *fit*.**"**

> MARGUERITE *reacts acidly to the wrong inflection and flounces out up* L.
>
> AMBROSE *follows her off.*

FIONA. **Wasn't she gorgeous. I'd give anything to look like that.**
NIGEL. **I think you are much nicer as you are.**
FIONA. **Oh, Nigel, that's the sweetest thing you've ever said to me.**

> AMBROSE *enters up* L *and crosses to* L *of Rowena.*

ROWENA. **Shall I go on, Mr Gusset?**
AMBROSE [*suffering*] **Yes, carry on, Rowena. You lack flow.**
ROWENA [*bridling*] **I'm sure I'm ever so sorry, Mr Gusset, but it's Flo's day off.**

> AMBROSE *backs above the sofa.*

[*She reads*] **"Here is Monica, who is going to show you an attractive design for the small miss."**
FIONA. **Ah, this is more in my line. I'm a small miss, aren't I?**
AMBROSE. **Titty-witty-witty, Mrs Tittlemouse. Get on with your** *Jemima Puddle Duck.*
ROWENA. **"We call this saucy little model 'Rufty-Tufty'."**

> ANTHEA, *a very tall, distinguished model enters up* C *to music played off. She carries a rolled umbrella and wears a pill-box hat with a fringe. She stands motionless as* ROWENA *continues to describe the wrong dress.*

MUSIC

"As you see, this model is in a carefree shade of irresolute apricot."

AMBROSE [*crossing to Rowena*] No, no, it's not—you don't know what you're saying. You've made a mistake.

ROWENA [*indignantly*] Well, that's what it says in the script. Don't ask me what an irresolute apricot looks like. You wrote it.

AMBROSE. But it isn't Monica.

ROWENA [*looking at Anthea*] Ooh, I'm ever so sorry, Mr Gusset. Ooh, I do feel a fool.

AMBROSE. Silly billy. [*He throws himself elegantly on the floor*]

ROWENA. "Ladies and gentlemen, Anthea will now present to you the ideal summer walking outfit."

ANTHEA *totters with extreme difficulty to* C.

AMBROSE [*rising and moving to* L *of Anthea*] Anthea, you have your hat on at quite the wrong angle, dear.

ANTHEA *stands still with a look of patient suffering.* AMBROSE *pulls the hat right over Anthea's eyes. She is now completely blinded.*

That's perfect—perfect! [*He turns to* L *of Rowena*]

ANTHEA *walks into Ambrose and nearly collides with the others on the sofa. Finally, using her umbrella as a blind man's stick, she hobbles out up* R.

JANE. Do you think we could see the evening dress next?

AMBROSE [*crossing down* R] See anything you like. The whole atmosphere's ruined. [*He collapses against the proscenium down* R]

ROWENA. "Now for our chef-doover."

FIONA. Our what?

ROWENA. "Here is a dress which only Gusset Creations *could* have produced."

AMBROSE *yelps.*

"We are lucky enough to have that famous vague muddle——"

AMBROSE *yelps.*

"—Vogue model—Zinia, to wear it for us. Ladies and gentlemen, Zinia—to show for us—'Effervescence'."

TROPPO *creeps into view and stands shyly in the entrance up* C.

JANE. Troppo!

AMBROSE *crawls to* C. TROPPO *runs to Jane and mimes frantically.* MARGUERITE *screams off* L *and runs on up* C. *She is in her corsets.* TIMOTHY *runs on after her.* MARGUERITE *runs down* R.

[*She rises*] Tim, what's happened?

FIONA *and* NIGEL *rise.*

TIMOTHY. It's Minnie. She's lost—*really* lost.

JANE. She can't be.

TIMOTHY. She's been stolen.

FIONA. Minnie! How terrible.

NIGEL. Minnie!

JANE. We must find her.

TIMOTHY. We'd better split up. You take Hyde Park—I'll take Kensington Gardens.

FIONA. Bags Battersea.

NIGEL. I'll come with you.

AMBROSE [*rising*] Rowena, fetch an ambulance.

ROWENA. Who do you think you are, and what do you think you're doing?

MUSIC

No. 14b

REPRISE

"WE'RE LOOKING FOR A PIANO"

ENSEMBLE

ALL. **We're looking for a piano,**
A piano? Yes, a piano.
AMBROSE. **Just any old pia . . . ?**
ALL. **No. The one that makes you gay.**
We have a sort of notion,
That a dash of sprightly motion
Is a stimulating potion
To be taken twice a day.

> TIMOTHY, TROPPO, JANE, FIONA, NIGEL, MARGUERITE *and* ROWENA *march round Ambrose and exit up* R, *singing as they go.*

We're look, look, look, etc. . . . .

> *The voices fade. The music continues.* AMBROSE *stands alone, a figure of monumental suffering.* ROWENA *enters up* R.

ROWENA. **Shall I make you a cup of tea, Mr Gusset? Are you feeling poorly?**
AMBROSE. **I'm drained of all emotions. I'm a husk. Leave me.**

> ROWENA *exits up* R. AMBROSE *weeps into his handkerchief.* ANTHEA *enters down* R, *still feeling her way with her umbrella. She bumps into* AMBROSE *who covers his face with his hands.* ANTHEA *lifts her hat for a moment to look, replaces it and leads* AMBROSE *out up* C, *he still with his face in his hands, she still tapping with the umbrella.*

> *The* RUNNING TABS *close*

SCENE 6

Frontcloth

The scene is played in front of the TABS.

> *The* TRAMP *enters* L, *crosses to* C *and stoops to pick up a fag-end.* JANE *enters* R. *She is breathless and very worried. She crosses to* L *of the Tramp then stops and turns. The lights come up for bright sunshine.*

LIGHTING CUE 27

JANE. **Excuse me, have you seen a piano anywhere—an old street piano?**

> *The* TRAMP *turns to Jane.*

It's you!
TRAMP [*calmly*] **So you've lost the piano.**
JANE. **I'm so sorry. It was stolen.**
TRAMP. **Stolen. Yes. It must be very difficult to guard a valuable possession every hour of the day.**
JANE. **But we** *did* **guard it, truly we did. I can't think how it happened.**
TRAMP. **No. You'd think a piano would be a difficult thing to steal.**
JANE. **We've failed you, haven't we? We'll return the money, of course.**
TRAMP. **The money's not important really, is it?**
JANE. **No, it's the piano.** [*With determination*] **We'll find her. Somehow we'll find her.**

TRAMP [*crossing to* L] **She's given you a lot of trouble. Perhaps I shouldn't have asked you**   MUSIC
to look after her in the first place.

JANE [*running to* R *of the Tramp*] **Oh, no, don't say that. I love Minnie dearly. She's made me happier than I've ever been before in my life.**

TRAMP. **Yes, she has that faculty. What has she done for** *you?* [*He sits down* L]

JANE [*kneeling* R *of the Tramp*] **She helped me to fall in love with my husband.**

TRAMP. **Timothy.**

JANE. **Yes. I'm waiting for him now. He should be here any minute, and between us we'll find Minnie.**

TRAMP. **I'm sure you will.**

JANE [*in amazement*] **You don't seem at all angry.**

TRAMP. **Angry! It's too hot to be angry.**

JANE. **It's a beautiful day.** [*She looks up at the sky*] **It hasn't rained for weeks.**

TRAMP. **Four weeks and two days. Today's the last day of the month.**

JANE. **What a month it's been.** [*She sings*]

SONG   No. 15

"THE TIME OF MY LIFE"

JANE

It's true I've been led an amazing dance,
But why should I ever complain?
If I could be given a second chance
I'd live it all over again.
Look at the weather and look at me
We're both in a summery haze
We're young and we're green as the leaf on the tree
For these are our salad days.

The RUNNING TABS *open.*

[*She rises and moves* LC]
Summer and sunshine and falling in love
All the sadness was foolish and vain.
It has melted away
In the heat of the day
And my heart is so full there's no room there for pain.

Summer and sunshine and falling in love
They can cut through despair like a knife.
There is joy in the air
So begone with dull care
I am having the time of my life.

The TRAMP *rises.*

This month has been enchanted
And it's all because of you,
For I have been transplanted
To a world that's exciting and new.

MUSIC

Summer and sunshine and falling in love
With a lover who made me his wife.
From my heart I can say
On this glorious day
I am having the time of my life.

The music continues. The TRAMP *mimes asking* JANE *to dance. She accepts. They dance.*

SCENE 7

The Park

JANE *and the* TRAMP *waltz gently to the music.*

JANE [*as they dance*] **If it's the last day of the month, we're due to return Minnie today.**
TRAMP. **I'll be back at four. By that time you'll have found her.**
JANE. **You have great faith in us.**
TRAMP. **Oh, yes. Good luck!**
JANE [*singing*]   **Summer and sunshine and falling in love**
With a lover who made me his wife.
From my heart I can say
On this glorious day
I'm so happy that I'm
In a mood so sublime
I am having the time of my life.

The TRAMP *bows and exits* R. JANE *moves* R *and waves after him.*

TIMOTHY *enters up* L.

TIMOTHY. **Jane, you were singing.** [*He crosses to* L *of Jane*] **How** *could* **you?**
JANE. **I'm sorry, Tim. I know I ought to be miserable, but I'm not. I've just seen the Tramp.**
TIMOTHY. **The Tramp? Does he know?**
JANE. **Yes, but he's not angry. He says he'll be back at four, and by that time he's sure we'll have found Minnie.**
TIMOTHY. **He's optimistic! I've had no luck so far.** [*He crosses to* L]

TROPPO *enters up* L *and comes down* C.

[*He moves to* L *of Troppo*] **Have you found her?**

TROPPO *shakes his head and cries.*

JANE [*moving to* R *of Troppo*] **Never mind.** [*She puts her arm around him*] **She can't be very far away.**
TIMOTHY. **If only someone would lend us a helicopter. We'd soon spot her then.**
JANE. **Surely you have an uncle who's an aviator?**
TIMOTHY [*seriously*] **No, I haven't, actually.**

TIMOTHY *sees* JANE *is laughing at him.*

Jane! Really! At a time like this.
JANE. **Sorry.**

The stage suddenly begins to go dark.

LIGHTING CUE

TIMOTHY [*looking up*] **Gosh, the evenings do seem to be drawing in.**
JANE. **But it's only three o'clock.**
TIMOTHY. **It must be a thunderstorm coming.**
JANE [*shading her eyes*] **It looks more like an eclipse to me.** [*She points upwards*] **Yes, look!**
There's a sort of shadow passing over the sun.
TIMOTHY [*nervously*] **It's—it's getting bigger, isn't it?**
JANE. **And it seems to be coming closer.**

> *A strange whirring sound is heard in the far distance.*

Timothy!
TIMOTHY. **Yes?**
JANE. **I think I'm rather frightened.**
TIMOTHY [*terrified*] **Oh, come, Jane. What is there to be afraid of?**

> *The noise increases, the stage grows darker.* TIMOTHY *and* JANE *cling to each other.* TROPPO *puts his head right inside his coat. The noise becomes deafening.*

JANE [*shouting*] **Tim!**
TIMOTHY. **Yes?**
JANE. **I love you.**
TIMOTHY. **What?**
JANE. **I love you.**
TIMOTHY. **I can't hear you.**

LIGHTING CUE 29
LIGHTING CUE 30

> *All three crouch on the ground as the noise reaches its climax. The stage goes completely dark. There is silence. The* LIGHTS *come up.* TIMOTHY *and* JANE *are on the ground,* TROPPO, *with an arm around each, protecting them. Behind them stands* ELECTRODE, *a man from Planet Zed. He is dressed in traditional space costume and has long blond hair. The others do not at first see him.*

[*He gets to his knees and slowly opens his eyes*] **There! It was only a thunderstorm passing overhead.**

> TIMOTHY *helps* JANE *to her feet.* TROPPO *rises.*

JANE. **More of an eclipse, you mean.**
TIMOTHY. **Don't be ridiculous, Jane. Eclipses don't make a noise.**

> TROPPO, *looking front, moves* RC.

JANE. **Thunderstorms usually rain.**
TIMOTHY [*laughing with relief*] **Well, whatever it was there was no need for you to be so frightened.**

> TROPPO *wanders up* R, *looking off* R.

JANE **Me? I wasn't the only one who was frightened.**

> *They dust themselves, rather deliberately looking away from each other.* JANE *is* RC. TIMOTHY *is* LC. ELECTRODE *is standing impassively* C, *just above them.*

TIMOTHY. **It isn't a question of** *courage.* **It's just that some people are afraid and some aren't.**
JANE [*lightly*] **How lucky for the "aren'ts".**
TIMOTHY [*turning and speaking straight to Electrode*] **There's no need to bring my aunts into it.**
[*He turns away without registering, and arranges his tie*] **I say, Jane, I don't care much for your new hair style.**
JANE. **What new hair style?**

Cut
to p 5

TIMOTHY. **All that Diana Dors stuff. I liked you better as you were.**

> TROPPO *moves down* R *and sees Electrode.*

JANE. **What** *are* **you talking about? I haven't changed my hair style for ages.**

> *It slowly dawns on* TIMOTHY *that it was not Jane he spoke to. He turns slowly, sees Electrode and faints dead away.* TROPPO *signals to* JANE *who turns, sees Electrode and jumps into* TROPPO's *arms. She recovers and takes a step towards Electrode.*

You've come from Outer Space.

> ELECTRODE *nods genially.*

However did you get here?

> ELECTRODE *points off* R.

[*She looks off* R *and gasps*] **Of course! I should have guessed. You came by saucer.**

> TROPPO *moves up* C.

[*She runs to Timothy and shakes him*] **Tim! Wake up! The Spaceman cometh.**
  TIMOTHY [*opening his eyes*] **I've just had a terrible dream.**

> JANE *pulls* TIMOTHY *to his feet.*

JANE. **No, you didn't. Look!**

> TIMOTHY *looks at Electrode and turns quickly away.* TROPPO *moves to* R *of Electrode.*

TIMOTHY. **Ugh!**
JANE. **That wasn't a thunderstorm or an eclipse—it was a saucer. He's come from Outer Space, Tim.**
  TIMOTHY [*groaning*] **I wish he'd go back there.**
JANE. **No. He's very nice. Look at his lovely hair and his wonderful smooth skin.**

> ELECTRODE *responds to the flattery, and smiles at Troppo.*

Troppo, I think he likes you. Ask him if he's friendly.

> ELECTRODE *makes signs to* TROPPO *who mimes to Timothy that Electrode wants to give him a message.*

[*To Timothy*] **He wants to speak with you.**
  TIMOTHY. **But I shan't be able to understand him.**
JANE [*grabbing Timothy*] **Of course you will.** [*She passes Timothy across the front of herself to* L *of Electrode*] **He'll do it by telepathy.**
  TIMOTHY. **But I can't speak telepathy.**

> ELECTRODE *prepares for telepathic communication by attaching various valves to Timothy.*

JANE. **Now, Tim, relax.**

> ELECTRODE *indicates that he is about to start.* TIMOTHY *grits his teeth and shuts his eyes.* ELECTRODE *concentrates very hard. One can see his brain working. There is a pause then a violent tremor passes through* TIMOTHY.

[*She grabs Timothy*] **Tim! Are you all right?**

> *There is a pause.* TIMOTHY *opens his eyes.*

What did he say?
  TIMOTHY [*in wonder*] **"How do you do?"**

> JANE *claps her hands with excitement.* TIMOTHY *closes his eyes. Another tremor passes through him.*

MUSIC

"My name is 'Electrode'."

JANE. **What a difficult name.**

Another tremor passes through TIMOTHY.

TIMOTHY. **"Will you come into my saucer and have a cup of tea?"**

JANE. **Thank you very much. Do you own it yourself?**

Another tremor passes through TIMOTHY.

TIMOTHY. **"No. I'm only a saucer's apprentice."**

JANE. **Isn't it amazing, Tim? Does it hurt?**

TIMOTHY. **No. As a matter of fact, it's rather nice.** [*He closes his eyes*]

More tremors pass through TIMOTHY.

"My master is anxious to help you."

JANE. **Help us? In what way, I wonder."**

More tremors pass through TIMOTHY.

TIMOTHY. **"A flying saucer is as good as a helicopter any day." What on earth does he mean by that?**

JANE. **Tim, don't you remember? You said, "If only we had a helicopter". They're going to help us to look for Minnie.**

TIMOTHY. **How wonderful!**

JANE [*crossing to* R *of Electrode*] **Can we start straight away?**

A tremor passes through TIMOTHY.

TIMOTHY. **"Yes, and here is my master to escort you to the saucer."**

UNCLE ZED *enters up* R. *He wears an outsize space helmet.* JANE *hides behind Troppo.* TIMOTHY *screams and runs off* L. UNCLE ZED *removes the helmet.*

TIMOTHY *re-enters.*

UNCLE ZED [*moving down* LC] **How do you do, Timothy?**

TIMOTHY. **Oh, hullo.**

JANE [*emerging*] **You know him?**

TIMOTHY. **Of course. He's my uncle. Uncle Zed, this is . . .**

UNCLE ZED. **No, no, my dear boy. You don't need to introduce us. I know already who this young lady is. How are you, Jane?**

JANE [*crossing to* R *of Uncle Zed and shaking hands*] **How did you guess we needed your help?**

UNCLE ZED. **It wasn't a guess, my dear. I can see and hear anything I want to on my panuro-scopo-telecinerama refracto vistavision set.** [*He hands his helmet to Jane*]

JANE *hands the helmet to Electrode.*

Now, hurry into the saucer—there's not a moment to lose. Electrode!

ELECTRODE *leaps to attention and salutes.*

Start the engines.

UNCLE ZED *exits up* R.

TIMOTHY. **There you see, I told you I had an uncle who was a high-up scientist.**

TROPPO *takes the helmet from Electrode and puts it on.*

JANE. **Yes, but I never thought he'd be as high up as that.**

JANE *and* TIMOTHY *exit up* R.

ELECTRODE. **Mind the doors, please.**

TROPPO *and* ELECTRODE, *arm in arm, exit up* R *as—*

the RUNNING TABS *close*

MUSIC

SCENE 8

Frontcloth

The scene is played in front of the RUNNING TABS.

NIGEL *enters* R, *pulling* FIONA *after him. He stops and turns.* FIONA *bumps into him. They are breathless.*

NIGEL. **We seem to have lost them completely.**

FIONA. **If I'd known we were going to do all this running about, I'd have put on my brogues.** [*She leans on Nigel's shoulder and removes her shoes*]

NIGEL [*depressed*] **She's probably in jail by now.**

FIONA. **Minnie?**

NIGEL. **No—Jane.**

FIONA. **You really mind about her, don't you?**

NIGEL. **Yes, of course.**

FIONA. **I'm so glad, because I mind about her, too. She is my best friend. And so** *pretty.* **But, darling, she has one serious drawback which I think you ought to know about.**

NIGEL. **What?**

FIONA. **She's** *married.*

NIGEL. **I know.**

FIONA. **You know? And it doesn't make any difference?**

NIGEL. **None at all. You see, I'm a friend of the family.**

FIONA. **Do you think I might become a friend of the family, too?**

NIGEL. **If you help them to find Minnie you'll be their friend for life.**

FIONA. **Oh, you darling.** [*She embraces him*] **There must be somebody we can ask.**

The TRAMP *enters* R, *crosses nonchalantly whistling to* L, *and picks up a fag-end.*

NIGEL. **How about** *him?*

The TRAMP *sits on the pros seat* L.

FIONA [*snobbishly*] **Oh, no! He's a** *tramp.*

NIGEL. **I'll ask him, all the same.** [*He crosses to the Tramp and taps him on the shoulder*] **Excuse me —we're looking for a boy, a girl and a piano.**

FIONA *crosses to* R *of Nigel.*

TRAMP. **Is that the name of a film?**

NIGEL. **No, I'm serious. It's a** *street* **piano. Sort of Victorian, I should think.**

FIONA. **Very grubby looking.** [*She puts on her shoes*]

NIGEL. **Quite a monstrosity, really.**

FIONA. **You might call it a hurdy-gurdy.**

TRAMP [*rising and crossing to* C] **Oh, no, you might not.**

FIONA. **I beg your pardon?**

TRAMP. **That would not be accurate.**

NIGEL. **You** *know* **the piano, then?**

TRAMP. **I may do.**

NIGEL. **Then will you help us to search?**

TRAMP. **Well, I'm not doing anything in particular at the moment. Yes, I'll help.**

FIONA [*moving to* L *of the Tramp*] **Oh, you** *darling.* [*She kisses him*]

NIGEL. **Have you** *any* **idea where the piano might be?**

TRAMP. **I have a hunch she's not very far away.**

FIONA. **And Jane and Timothy? Where are they?**

TRAMP. **If you want my candid opinion, Jane and Timothy have vanished into space.**

NIGEL, FIONA *and the* TRAMP *exit* L.

SCENE 9

The Flying Saucer

It is an attractive saucer with a delicate, floral design round the rim. It is tipped slightly towards the audience so that this is visible. There is a small, low table C, and three small stools, R, L and above the table.

> *When the* RUNNING TABS *open,* UNCLE ZED *is seated above the table,* TIMOTHY *is seated* R *of it and* JANE *is seated* L *of it. They are having tea.* TROPPO *is seated on the floor below Jane, wearing the helmet.* ELECTRODE *is seated below the table, paddling the saucer through the air with a large teaspoon.*

TRIO   **No. 16**

"THE SAUCER SONG"

JANE, TIMOTHY *and* UNCLE ZED

> *During the opening verse,* JANE, TIMOTHY *and* UNCLE ZED *tap out the rhythm on their saucers with teaspoons.* TROPPO *removes his helmet, puts it aside, picks up a telescope, leans over the edge of the saucer and looks for the piano.*

JANE, TIMOTHY *and* UNCLE ZED.

> **It might have been a flying plate,**
> **Or perhaps a flying dish,**
> **A flying cup or a flying spoon**
> **Or even a flying fish.**
> **But of all the many things that fly**
> **By Nature or by Art**
> **You'll find a flying saucer**
> **Will get off to a flying start.**

UNCLE ZED *rises.*

UNCLE ZED.

> **You never saw a saucer,**
> **So saucy as mine.**
> **You never saw a saucer**
> **That's even half as fine.**
> **What a joy and pride**
> **It is to ride**
> **Upon my astral courser.**
> **Oh, aren't I clever?**
> **Nobody ever**
> **Saw such a saucy saucer.**

JANE *and* TIMOTHY *rise.*

JANE *and* TIMOTHY

> **Oh, isn't he clever?**
> **Nobody ever**
> **Saw such a saucy saucer.**

JANE *and* TIMOTHY *sit.*

UNCLE ZED.

> I hate these modern air machines
> All smart and streamy-lined.
> Give me a dear old saucer
> That's hand-painted and refined.
> Some choose the Willow Pattern type.
> Crown Derby's pretty rare
> But mine is quite a special line
> In flying saucer ware.
>
> You never saw a saucer
> So saucy as mine.
> You never saw a saucer
> So cosy in design.
> She loves to fly
> Beyond the sky,
> And no-one has to force her
> Oh, aren't I clever?
> Nobody ever
> Saw such a saucy saucer.

JANE *and* TIMOTHY *rise.*

JANE. *and* TIMOTHY.

> Oh, isn't he clever?
> Nobody ever
> Saw such a saucy saucer.

UNCLE ZED, JANE *and* TIMOTHY *resume their seats.* TROPPO *puts down the telescope.* ELECTRODE *moderates his paddling and only occasionally twists his spoon.*

TIMOTHY. Tell me, Uncle Zed, what exactly is your job?

UNCLE ZED. I'm an astral navigator.

JANE. You must see some very interesting sights.

UNCLE ZED. Oh, yes. Some of those Venus girls are delightful. I fell in love with one of them once.

JANE. Why didn't you marry her?

UNCLE ZED [*sadly*] I was under a Venusian delusion.

JANE. You poor thing. Why?

UNCLE ZED. She was secretly married to a planetary inspector.

JANE. How dreadful!

UNCLE ZED. Yes. For a while I was inconsolable. And then the most exciting thing happened.

TIMOTHY. What?

UNCLE ZED. I discovered a new planet.

TIMOTHY. What did you call it?

UNCLE ZED. Planet Zed.

TIMOTHY. Was it uninhabited?

UNCLE ZED. No, full of people.

JANE. *Nice* people?

UNCLE ZED [*patting Electrode's hand*] Charming.

JANE. Any pleasures and pastimes?

UNCLE ZED. Hunting, shooting and nuclear fission.

JANE. But doesn't it sound *lovely*, Tim? Perhaps we could go there for our honeymoon?

TIMOTHY. Yes, let's. But not until we find Minnie.

JANE'S *face falls.* TROPPO *picks up the telescope and looks through it.*

JANE. **Minnie. I'd forgotten about her.**
TIMOTHY. **Any sign of her, Troppo?**

TROPPO *shakes his head.*

[*He rises*] **Here, let me have a look.** [*He takes the telescope from Troppo and looks through it to* R] **Gosh, what a view—how beautiful London looks.** [*He directs the telescope at the top of Electrode's head*] **There's the dome of St Paul's. I've never seen the Thames look so** *clean.* **There's the Albert Hall, and there's . . . Jane! Look, Jane!**
JANE [*rising*] **What is it?**
TIMOTHY. **I do believe . . .** [*He hands the telescope to Jane*] **Look.**

UNCLE ZED *rises.*

JANE [*looking through the telescope*] **It is! It is! It's Minnie. I'd know her anywhere.**
TIMOTHY. **Uncle Zed, can we land at once?**
UNCLE ZED. **No, no. To ground a flying saucer twice in one day might cause comment. We'll bale out. Electrode, dip the saucer.**

ELECTRODE *flails the air with his spoon.*

REPRISE

No. 16a

"THE SAUCER SONG"

JANE, TIMOTHY *and* UNCLE ZED

UNCLE ZED.	**You never saw a saucer**
	So saucy as mine.
	You never saw a saucer
	That's even half as fine.
ALL.	**She's firmly wed**
	To Uncle Zed
	And [I] will not divorce her
	** [he]**
	Oh, [aren't I] clever?
	** [isn't he]**
	Nobody ever
	Saw such a saucy saucer.

LIGHTING CUE 31

The LIGHTS BLACK-OUT *as—*
the RUNNING TABS *close*

SCENE 10

Frontcloth

The scene is played in front of the RUNNING TABS.

LIGHTING CUE 32

When the LIGHTS *come up,* TIMOTHY'S MOTHER *enters* L *and* LADY RAEBURN *enters* R. *They see each other and stop,* TIMOTHY'S MOTHER LC *and* LADY RAEBURN *at* RC.

DUET

"WE DON'T UNDERSTAND OUR CHILDREN"

TIMOTHY'S MOTHER *and* LADY RAEBURN

LADY RAEBURN [*over the music*] **There's Timothy's mother.**
TIMOTHY'S MOTHER. **There's Jane's mother.**
LADY RAEBURN
TIMOTHY'S MOTHER } [*together*] **Oh, dear! I can't get away now—she's seen me. Oh dear!**
LADY RAEBURN [*singing*] **She'll ask after Jane.**
TIMOTHY'S MOTHER.   **She'll ask after Tim.**
BOTH.   **Oh, what can I say—**
LADY RAEBURN.   **About her?**
TIMOTHY'S MOTHER   **About him?**
BOTH.   **She's certain to guess my inward distress.**
                 Oh what a relief it would be to confess
                 That—
                     They come together.

We don't understand our children,
We hardly know the things they do.
We think they used to heed us,
To love us and to need us
But never since the age of two.
We wanted to be enlightened
Improving as we went along,
But it always seems too late
To be really up-to-date
And we still contrive to do things wrong.

We've tried not to possess them,
To twist them or suppress them,
Observing every rule since they were small.
We've shown determination
In adjusting our relation
And we feel we're not related now at all.

We don't understand our children.
We've tried to follow all the modern trends
And we know they don't enjoy
Being mummy's girl or boy
So d'you think they'd let us be just friends?

TIMOTHY'S MOTHER.   **Don't ask after Tim.**
LADY RAEBURN.   **Don't ask after Jane**
BOTH.   **We'll make it a pact not to do so again.**
                 But just for this once we'll say what is true
                 It's such a relief to confess it to you,
                 That—
                 They link arms.

We don't understand our children
Our knowledge has become confused.
For since the age of four,
They've taught us so much more
That we're bewildered and bemused.
We know that we must not spoil them,
We've tried to follow all the modern trends,
But they've flouted or destroyed
All the things we learnt from Freud
Oh, d'you think they'd let us be just friends?

LADY RAEBURN *and* TIMOTHY'S MOTHER *exit together* R.

SCENE 11

The Park

When the RUNNING TABS *open, the piano is* C. BOOT *is standing* LC *and* WILLIAMS *is standing* RC.

BOOT. **There she stands, sir.**
WILLIAMS [*moving above the piano*] **Well done, Boot, well done.**
BOOT. **Thank you, sir.**
WILLIAMS [*crossing to* R *of Boot*] **I'll see you get promotion for this.**
BOOT. **Oh, thank you, sir.**
WILLIAMS. **Well, she's prominent enough—the owners won't have any difficulty in finding her now. Then we have them all together.**
BOOT. **It's a piece of cake, sir.**
WILLIAMS. **I say, Boot, while there's nobody about, how about trying her out?**
BOOT [*puzzled*] **Sir?**
WILLIAMS. **Oh, come now, don't you play at all?**
BOOT. **No, sir. Not a note, sir.**
WILLIAMS. **Nothing? Not even the** *Bluebells of Scotland Yard?* [*He goes up* L *and looks off* R]

BOOT *blows his whistle and beckons off* L.

ROWENA *enters* L. *She and* BOOT *crouch and hide below the piano.*

BOOT. **Did you hear that?**
ROWENA. **Promotion.**
BOOT. **I shall ask you to marry me.**
ROWENA. **Lancelot!**
BOOT. **And all I did was to come upon it, standing idle. Mind you, it's time I had a bit of luck—for the past month they've been passing the buck from one to another and it's always landed up with me.**
ROWENA. **You should have no truck with the buck.**

BOOT *kisses Rowena.*

LADY RAEBURN *and* TIMOTHY'S MOTHER *enter up* R.

BOOT [*peeping over the piano*] **Somebody's coming—take cover.**

BOOT *and* ROWENA *move the piano* L *and hide behind it.*

TIMOTHY'S MOTHER. **Augustine!**

LADY RAEBURN. **Mr Williams!**

WILLIAMS. **Aaah! Lady Raeburn.** [*He moves to* L *of Lady Raeburn and kisses her hand*] **Good afternoon.** [*To Timothy's Mother*] **Hello, Sis.** [*He kisses her*]

TIMOTHY'S MOTHER. **Strolling in the park?**

LADY RAEBURN. **Is Parliament resting?**

WILLIAMS. **Tossing in its sleep, Lady Raeburn, on account of a piano.**

TIMOTHY'S MOTHER. **A piano?**

WILLIAMS. **Yes.** [*He points*] **There it stands. People dance to it, I believe, on quite a grand scale.**

LADY RAEBURN, TIMOTHY'S MOTHER *and* WILLIAMS *move down* RC.

TIMOTHY'S MOTHER. **And the people who play the piano, who are they?**

WILLIAMS. **I'm afraid, ladies, you're in for a nasty shock.**

LADY RAEBURN. **A** *nasty* **one?**

TIMOTHY, JANE *and* TROPPO *enter up* L *and rush to the piano.*

WILLIAMS. **Where are your children, at the moment?**

TIMOTHY'S MOTHER. **Oh, we've no idea.**

LADY RAEBURN. **We don't understand our children.**

TIMOTHY'S MOTHER. **Good gracious me, here they are.**

JANE. **Timothy, it is, it is.**

TIMOTHY. **Jane!**

They bring the piano C.

TIMOTHY'S MOTHER. **Timothy!**

TIMOTHY. **Oh, hullo, Mother—not now.**

BOOT. **One moment, sir; one moment, miss. This vehicle is in my charge.**

BOOT *moves and stands above the piano.* ROWENA *moves to* L *of Boot.* TROPPO *stands down* L *of the piano.* TIMOTHY *and* JANE *stand up* R *of it.*

TIMOTHY ⎱
JANE ⎰ [*together*] **What?**

BOOT. **I will trouble you for your licence.**

TIMOTHY. **But I haven't got a licence.**

BOOT. **Then I arrest all three of you.** [*He moves below the piano*]

ROWENA *moves down* L.

LADY RAEBURN ⎱
TIMOTHY'S MOTHER ⎰ [*together*] **Oh!**

WILLIAMS. **I'm afraid, ladies, I have a very unpleasant duty to perform.** [*He moves to* R *of Timothy*]

TIMOTHY'S MOTHER. **Timothy, what did you do it for?**

TIMOTHY. **Seven pounds a week.**

LADY RAEBURN. **You mean you were being paid?**

JANE. **We took the hat round, too.**

UNCLE ZED *enters down* R.

LADY RAEBURN. **I shall never get over this, never.** [*She sees Uncle Zed*] **Oh, good afternoon.**

TIMOTHY'S MOTHER. **Why, Zed—it's you!**

UNCLE ZED [*kissing her*] **Hullo, Sis.**

TIMOTHY'S MOTHER. **I thought you'd disappeared from the face of the earth**

UNCLE ZED. **So I had. I've just baled out.**

TIMOTHY'S MOTHER. **Oh, don't talk about baling out.**

LADY RAEBURN [*holding out her hand*] **Won't somebody introduce me?**

UNCLE ZED *crosses and kisses Lady Raeburn's hand.*

BOOT [*to Timothy and Jane*] **Come along quietly, if you please.** [*He pushes Timothy and Jane to* L]

WILLIAMS. **Now, just a moment, Boot. I've told you before not to be so impulsive. I want to hear the instrument first.**

TIMOTHY. **Hear it?**
BOOT. **Oh, no, sir, please. It'll be your undoing.**
WILLIAMS. **Timothy, would you mind obliging?**
TIMOTHY [*delighted*] **Uncle Augustine, yes.** [*He moves to the piano*]
BOOT. **No, sir, no! I beg of you.**
WILLIAMS. **Quiet, Boot. Play, Timothy.**

> TIMOTHY *plays. At first,* JANE *and* TROPPO *dance a little from force of habit. Then they stop and look at* WILLIAMS, *who stands rigid.*

TIMOTHY [*as he plays*] **Dance, Uncle, dance, you old stick-in-the-mud. You're the only one she hasn't affected.**
WILLIAMS. **The only one?**

> TIMOTHY *stops playing and looks round. Everyone is motionless.*

JANE [*moving to* L *of Timothy*] **Play, Timothy, play.**

> TIMOTHY *plays again, discordant notes.*

WILLIAMS. **Take them away, Boot.**

> BOOT *moves to* L *of the piano.*

TIMOTHY. **What's happening. What's happening?**

> TROPPO *pushes Boot aside and opens the lid of the piano.*

What is it, Troppo? There's no inscription!
JANE. **It isn't Minnie.**
TIMOTHY. **It's a fake.** [*He moves* C] **There, you see? You haven't captured her at all. Who do you suppose put this here?**
JANE. **The Tramp. The Tramp. Only he could have thought of it.**
TIMOTHY. **But if this isn't Minnie, where is she?**

> *The sound of a piano is heard being played off* R.

REPRISE   No. 18

"OH, LOOK AT ME, I'M DANCING"

ENSEMBLE

Everyone begins to dance.

> FIONA *wheels "Minnie" on* R, *with the* TRAMP *playing and* NIGEL *carrying the stool. They set the piano* C *and the* TRAMP *sits on the stool.* TROPPO *pushes the duplicate piano off* L, *and re-enters.*

ALL [*singing and dancing*] **It isn't a thing I'm accustomed to do.**
    Oh, look at me! Oh, look at me!
    Oh, look at me! I'm dancing.
    Now who would have thought I'd behave in this way?
    It isn't a thing I do every day.
    It's nice for a change,
    And I'm happy to say,
    I'm dancing, dancing, dancing.

> *The* TRAMP *turns on the stool and faces front.*

JANE. **It's you!**
TIMOTHY. **It's you!**
UNCLE ZED. **It's you!**

                                                              MUSIC

WILLIAMS. **It's you!**

TIMOTHY'S MOTHER. **It's you!**

TIMOTHY. **You know him, Mother?**

TIMOTHY'S MOTHER. **Know him? He's your uncle.**

TIMOTHY laughs.

What are you laughing at, Tim? How can you? It's your Uncle Ba-Ba.

TRAMP. **The black sheep.**

TIMOTHY. **Of course. The one we don't mention.** [*He shakes hands with the Tramp*] **How do you do, sir?**

TRAMP. **We've met before.**

LADY RAEBURN. **Mr Williams, are you going through with this horrible prison thing?**

WILLIAMS [*skipping to* L] **I've been dancing, Lady Raeburn. I'm an accessory after the fact.**

TIMOTHY. **Uncle Augustine, you're actually smiling.**

WILLIAMS. **Yes, I'm feeling very gay.** [*He tries to kiss Rowena*]

BOOT moves between Williams and Rowena.

TIMOTHY. **There, you see. It was Minnie.**

TIMOTHY'S MOTHER. **It's all very well, feeling gay**—[*to the Tramp*] **but, Barnabas, what do you think you're at?**

TRAMP. **You told Timothy he was free to choose a profession from among his uncles.**

TIMOTHY'S MOTHER. **You call this a profession?**

TRAMP [*rising and crossing down* L] **Seven pounds a week.** [*He leans against the proscenium*]

TROPPO takes a bag of money out of the piano and stands below the piano,
clutching the bag.

TIMOTHY [*moving to* L *of Troppo*] **Oh, look! The collection.**

JANE [*moving to* L *of Timothy*] **It's enormous.** *I can't believe we've collected so much.*

TIMOTHY. **We must have a share out.**

JANE. **Most of it's in silver. It must be worth pounds.**

TIMOTHY. **Doesn't that make you feel better, Mother?**

TIMOTHY'S MOTHER. **A little, dear.**

TIMOTHY. **And you** *did* **enjoy dancing.**

TIMOTHY'S MOTHER. **Yes, dear, but what will you do in the winter?**

UNCLE ZED. **Come to Planet Zed.**

TROPPO replaces the bag in the piano and stands above it.

JANE. **Do you think we could get another temporary job there?**

UNCLE ZED. **Why not?** [*He puts an arm around Lady Raeburn*] **Everything's very romantic on Zed.**

LADY RAEBURN. **I** *wish* **somebody would introduce me.**

TIM. **Uncle Zed—this is Lady Raeburn.**

LADY RAEBURN [*to Uncle Zed*] **I'm giving a little party for my daughter. I wonder if you'd care to come along.**

JANE [*linking arms with Timothy*] **Mother, don't you think we'd better cancel it? You see, Timothy and I are married.**

LADY RAEBURN   } [*together*] { **Jane!**
TIMOTHY'S MOTHER }   { **Timothy!**

LADY RAEBURN. **And it was to have been at St Margaret's.**

JANE. **Never mind, darling. Perhaps St Margaret's will come in for** *you.*

LADY RAEBURN. **Oh, there's nothing left for me but to disappear from society.**

<small>UNCLE ZED and LADY RAEBURN cross to L. NIGEL and FIONA whisper
together then creep down R to the Tramp. TIMOTHY introduces Jane to his
mother. He then goes to WILLIAMS, takes him to Troppo and introduces them.
WILLIAMS sits on the piano stool. TIMOTHY stands L. of Williams. JANE
takes TIMOTHY'S MOTHER to Troppo and introduces them. They stand
above the piano. BOOT and ROWENA stand down L.</small>

UNCLE ZED [to Lady Raeburn] **The trip to Zed might prove to be most salutary. Would you** MUSIC
care to come?
LADY RAEBURN. **In a saucer? What does one wear for saucer travel?**
UNCLE ZED. **Just a tee shirt.**

LADY RAEBURN *and* UNCLE ZED *move up* LC.

FIONA [to Nigel] **Shall we?**
NIGEL. **Yes, let's.**
TRAMP. **Well?**
NIGEL. **Can we ask? Or do we have to wait to be asked?**

The TRAMP *takes out a bundle of notes and hands them to Nigel.*

[He counts the notes] **Twenty-eight pounds.**
FIONA. **Oh,** *thank* **you. Tell me, do all the people who look after Minnie get married?**
TRAMP. **I never did. She's all yours.**

FIONA *blows a kiss to the Tramp then moves to* R *of the piano.* NIGEL
follows to R *of Fiona.* UNCLE ZED *and* LADY RAEBURN *move down* RC.
TIMOTHY'S MOTHER *crosses to* L *of Uncle Zed.* JANE *moves to* L *of
Timothy.*

WILLIAMS [to Nigel] **Excuse me, sir, are you the new owner of the piano?**
NIGEL. **Temporarily—yes.**
WILLIAMS [rising] **Then I have a message for you.**
NIGEL. **A message?**
WILLIAMS. **From the Palace.** [He takes a letter from his pocket] **It's rather gay. I'll read it out.**
[He reads] **"The Master of the Royal Household is requested to command the presence of
the itinerant piano known as Minnie to entertain the guests on the occasion of the Royal
Garden Party." And that occasion, ladies and gentlemen, is this afternoon.**
FIONA [after a pause] **Nigel!** [She embraces Nigel]

WILLIAMS *moves* LC.

This is, without exception, the happiest day I have ever had in the whole of my life.
NIGEL. **But Tim and Jane ought to go.**

All look at Timothy and Jane.

FIONA. **Of** *course.* **Jane . . .**
JANE. **No.**
LADY RAEBURN. **Jane,** *darling!*
TIMOTHY'S MOTHER. **Timothy, you** *must.*
TIMOTHY. **No. The piano isn't ours now. Our month's over.**
JANE. *Really,* **Fiona.**
FIONA. **Oh, thank you. Thank you.**

TROPPO *moves and sits on the piano stool.*

NIGEL. **Are we to manage without Troppo?**
JANE. **Troppo—you can go with Minnie or you can stay with us. Which would you rather?**

TROPPO *rises, looks from one to the other, then puts his hand on the piano.*

Go with Minnie, then. Thank you for everything. [She crosses and kisses Troppo]
WILLIAMS [skipping to Timothy's Mother] **Well, shall I lead the way to the Palace?**
NIGEL [before venturing to sit at the piano] **Jane?**
JANE. **Yes.** [She turns to Fiona] **Good luck, Fiona.** [She kisses her]
FIONA. **Thank you.**
TIMOTHY [shaking hands with Nigel] **Good luck, Nigel.**

NIGEL. **Thanks.**
TIMOTHY. **I say, I hope you can play.**

> NIGEL *sits at the piano.* JANE *and* TIMOTHY *turn their backs on the others and stay in that position until everyone has gone. The* TRAMP *still stands down* R.

NIGEL. **I say, I don't think I can.**
FIONA [L *of Nigel*] **Of course you can play.**

REPRISE   No. 19

"OH LOOK AT ME, I'M DANCING"

ENSEMBLE

> NIGEL *plays.*

NIGEL [*over the music*] **Yes, I . . . No, I can't. Yes, I can. Oh, look at me! I'm playing.** [*He* **rises**]

> *As* NIGEL *plays,* FIONA *begins to push the piano off.* TROPPO *picks up the stool and follows. The others sing and dance off after them,* LADY RAEBURN *with* UNCLE ZED, TIMOTHY'S MOTHER *with* WILLIAMS *and* BOOT *with* ROWENA.

ALL [*singing*]   It isn't a thing I'm accustomed to do.
Oh, look at me! Oh, look at me!
Oh, look at me! I'm dancing.
Now who would have thought I'd behave in this way?
It isn't a thing I do every day.
It's nice for a change, and I'm happy to say,
I'm dancing, dancing, dancing.

I'm going backwards instead of forwards,
I'm spinning like a top.
I'm going sideways, I'm going upwards,
I doubt if I can stop.
Oh, look at me! Oh, look at me!
Oh, look at me! I'm dancing!
My feet are so wayward they've got out of hand,
I leap in the air never hoping to land.
I'm gay and I'm breathless and jubilant
And I'm dancing, dancing, dancing.

> *The voices die away. The* TRAMP *moves slowly up* R.

JANE. **Oh, Tim!**
TIMOTHY [*putting his arm around her*] **I know.**
TRAMP [*up* C] **Don't look back.**
JANE [*without looking round*] **You're still there.**
TIMOTHY. **Don't look back.**

> *The* TRAMP *exits slowly up* L.

REPRISE

"WE SAID WE WOULDN'T LOOK BACK"

JANE *and* TIMOTHY

JANE.	If I start looking behind me
	And begin retracing my track
	I'll remind you to remind me
BOTH.	We said we wouldn't look back.
TIMOTHY.	And if you should happen to find me
	With an outlook dreary and black
	I'll remind you to remind me,
BOTH.	We said we wouldn't look back.

LIGHTING CUE 33

JANE *and* TIMOTHY, *with their arms around each other, exit slowly up* R *as the* LIGHTS *dim to* BLACK-OUT *and—*

the CURTAIN *falls*

FURNITURE AND PROPERTY LIST

ACT I

Scene 1

On stage: Piano. *On it:* 2 oil lamps, lamp with red glasses
          In it: bundle of notes, slip of paper
        Piano stool

Off stage: Coin (DON)
        Scroll for Jane (FEMALE DON)
        Scroll for Timothy (DON)

Scene 2

On stage: Window flat with curtains and pelmet
        Round table. *On it:* white cloth, cups, saucers,
        teaspoons, small plates, 2 newspapers, toast,
        marmalade, knives, honey, comic, jug of
        milk, pot of tea, sugar basin, jam, bread

Off stage: Chair (FATHER)
        Chair (MOTHER)
        Chair (AUNT PRUE)

Personal: TIMOTHY: packet of cigarettes, matches

Scene 3

On stage: 2 park chairs

Off stage: Book (TIMOTHY)
        Piano cover (TRAMP)
        Packet of sandwiches (TRAMP)
        Beer bottle (TRAMP)

Personal: JANE: watch
        TIMOTHY: handkerchief, glasses

Scene 4

On stage: Hairdresser's swivel chair
        Portable hair dryer
        Trolley. *On it:* towel for turban, 2 pots of cold

cream, tissues, face pack mask, mascara and
brush, rouge and puff, powder and puff

Off stage: White telephone with long lead (HELOISE)
        Tray. *On it:* manicure materials, bowl of water
        (MANICURIST)
        Telephone (MANICURIST)

Scene 5

Setting as SCENE 3

On stage: 1 park chair (RC)

Off stage: Dress box marked "Gusset Creations" (ROWENA)
        Book (BISHOP)

Personal: BOOT: police whistle
        BISHOP: coin
        TROPPO: hat

Scene 6

On stage: Desk. *On it:* vase of flowers, papers
        Desk chair
        Safe. *In it:* tray with pot of tea, sugar basin,
        milk jug, 3 each cups, saucers and teaspoons

Off stage: Chair (FOSDYKE)

Personal: UNCLE CLAM: hat, umbrella
        FOSDYKE: hat
        TIMOTHY: hat

Scene 7

On stage: High desk. *On it:* large book, pen
        Gramophone and records
        In gramophone cupboard: ballet shoes

Scene 8

Off stage: Piano. *In it:* packet of sandwiches
        Newspaper (NIGEL)

ACT II

Scene 1

On stage: Stool (up C)
        Gong on stand (up LC)
        Upright piano. *On it:* table-lamp
        Table (down R) *On it:* cloth, glasses
        Table (up L) *On it:* cloth, table-lamp, glasses,
        camera
        Table (down L) *On it:* cloth, table-lamp, glasses
        6 upright chairs

Stand microphone

Off stage: Tray. *On it:* bottle of champagne in cooler
        (WAITRESS)
        Tray. *On it:* plate of egg and chips

Personal: SLAVE: wrist-watch
        GIRL ARMS DANCER: handkerchief, cigarette
        MAN ARMS DANCER: matches

71

Scene 2

Off stage: Piano

Scene 3

On stage: Café table. (RC) *On it:* comic, glass of ice-cream soda, 2 straws

Off stage: 2 chairs
Towel (TIMOTHY)
Ice-cream soda (TROPPO)

Personal: JANE: watch
WILLIAMS: umbrella
TIMOTHY: dark glasses

Scene 4

No properties

Scene 5

On stage: 2 tall stands. *On them:* vases of flowers
Armchair (RC)
Sofa (LC) *On it:* cushions
On stand RC: books, sweets, scent spray

Off stage: Feather duster (AMBROSE)
List of dresses (ROWENA)
Umbrella (ANTHEA)

Personal: AMBROSE: handkerchief

Scene 6

No properties

Scene 7

Personal: ELECTRODE: valves

Scene 8

No properties

Scene 9

In saucer: 3 stools
Telescope
Large spoon
Table. *On it:* 3 cups, saucers, teaspoons

Scene 10

No properties

Scene 11

On stage: Duplicate piano

Off stage: Piano. *In it:* bag of money (TRAMP)

Personal: BOOT: whistle
TRAMP: bundle of notes
WILLIAMS: letter

MADE AND PRINTED IN GREAT BRITAIN BY
LATIMER TREND & COMPANY LTD PLYMOUTH
MADE IN ENGLAND

LIGHTING PLOT

ACT I, SCENE 1. Exterior
To open: General lighting dim
Pool of light c to cover area around piano

Cue 1   The TRAMP rises   (Page 1)
Bring up general lighting for sunshine effect

Cue 2   At end of Scene   (Page 5)
Dim lights to BLACK-OUT

ACT I, SCENE 2. Interior
Cue 3   When Scene is set   (Page 5)
Bring up lights to cover inset C

Cue 4   MOTHER blows out match   (Page 7)
Dim lights to BLACK-OUT

ACT I, SCENE 3. Exterior
Cue 5   When Scene is set   (Page 8)
Bring up general lighting for sunshine effect

Cue 6   At end of Scene as JANE whirls   (Page 15)
Dim lights to BLACK-OUT

ACT I, SCENE 4. Interior
Cue 7   When Scene is set   (Page 15)
Bring up lights to cover inset C

Cue 8   HELOISE applies cream to Lady Raeburn's nose   (Page 18)
Dim lights to BLACK-OUT

ACT I, SCENE 5. Exterior
Cue 9   When Scene is set   (Page 18)
Bring up lights for sunshine effect

Cue 10   When CHORUS exit in front of TABS   (Page 22)
Dim lights to BLACK-OUT

ACT I, SCENE 6. Interior
Cue 11   When TABS open   (Page 23)
Bring up lights

Cue 12   UNCLE CLAM, FOSDYKE and TIMOTHY
exit   (Page 26)
Dim lights to BLACK-OUT

ACT I, SCENE 7. Interior
Cue 13   When TABS open   (Page 26)
Bring up lights

Cue 14   The INSPECTOR holds up ballet shoes   (Page 29)
Dim lights to BLACK-OUT

ACT I, SCENE 8. Exterior
Cue 15   Follows previous cue after RUNNING
TABS are closed   (Page 29)
Bring up lights for early evening effect

Cue 16   TIMOTHY plays   (Page 31)
Snap in street lamp effect

ACT II, SCENE 1. Exterior/Interior
To open: The stage in darkness
Cue 17   At rise of CURTAIN   (Page 33)
Spotlight on MANAGER *at doorway* c

Cue 18   When RUNNING TABS open   (Page 34)
Bring up subdued lighting on Club interior
Bring in table-lamps
Take out spotlight

Cue 19   SLAVE strikes gong   (Page 35)
Dim lights a little
Spotlight focuses on ARMS DANCERS *up* c

Cue 20   When ARMS DANCER strangles GIRL   (Page 35)
BLACK-OUT

Cue 21   After DANCERS exit   (Page 35)
Bring up lights as Cue 18

Cue 22   At end of Scene as RUNNERS close   (Page 38)
BLACK-OUT

ACT II, SCENE 2. Exterior
Cue 23   Follows previous cue after RUNNING
TABS are closed   (Page 38)
Bring up lights for night effect

Cue 24   TIMOTHY, NIGEL and JANE exit   (Page 42)
Dim lights to BLACK-OUT

ACT II, SCENE 3. Exterior
Cue 25   When RUNNING TABS open   (Page 42)
Bring up lights for sunshine effect

ACT II, SCENE 4. Exterior
No cues

ACT II, SCENE 5. Interior
Cue 26   When RUNNING TABS open   (Page 50)
Cross fade lights for interior effect

ACT II, SCENE 6. Exterior
Cue 27   JANE enters   (Page 53)
Bring up lights for bright sunshine effect

ACT II, SCENE 7. Exterior
Cue 28   JANE: "Sorry."   (Page 55)
Commence slow dim of all lights

Cue 29   TIMOTHY: "I can't hear you."   (Page 56)
BLACK-OUT

Cue 30   Follows above cue   (Page 56)
Bring up lights as at the opening of the scene

ACT II, SCENE 8. Exterior
No cues

ACT II, SCENE 9. Exterior
To open: Pool of light on flying saucer inset C
Cue 31   At end of Scene   (Page 62)
Dim lights to BLACK-OUT

ACT II, SCENE 10. Exterior
Cue 32   Follows previous cue after RUNNING
TABS closed   (Page 62)
Bring up lights for sunshine effect

ACT II, SCENE 11. Exterior
Cue 33   JANE and TIMOTHY exit   (Page 70)
Dim lights to BLACK-OUT

EFFECTS PLOT

ACT I

ACT II

The University

The Breakfast-room

The Park

The Foreign Office

The Beauty Parlour

The Inspector's Office

The Night Club

The Dress Shop

The Flying Saucer